Youth Cells and Youth Ministry

Discipling the Postmodern Generations

A ministry of DOVE Christian Fellowship International
Ephrata, Pennsylvania USA

Youth Cells and Youth Ministry

Compiled by Brian Sauder & Sarah Mohler

Authors: Shawn & Joanna Eberly, Hubie Harmon, Sarah Mohler, Brian Sauder, Bill Toombs

© Revised edition 2000
Copyright © 1997
House to House Publications
1924 West Main Street, Ephrata, PA 17522
Telephone: (717) 738-3751
FAX: (717) 738-0656

ISBN 1-886973-33-4

Unless otherwise noted, all scripture quotations are taken from the New International Version of the Bible, © 1973, 1978, 1984 by International Bible Society.

Contents

Authors

This book, compiled by Brian Sauder and Sarah Mohler, has five contributing authors:

Brian Sauder serves on the DOVE Christian Fellowship International (DCFI) Apostolic Council. He and his wife, Janet, have led many youth cells. Brian is currently involved in leadership training.

Sarah Mohler is a youth resource person of DCFI and works with the Ephrata/Lititz junior and senior high youth groups. She has been a youth cell leader for 13 years.

Shawn and Joanna Eberly served as youth leaders, covering the youth cells as well as the youth and post high groups at Ephrata/ Lititz DCFI for several years. They currently are youth pastors in New Zealand.

Hubie Harmon has been a youth resource person of DCFI for 10 years. He pastors the Lebanon DCFI youth group and oversees several youth cells there. Hc also founded and leads Koinonia Connection Ministries, an urban ministry in Philadelphia.

Bill Toombs is the assistant pastor of India-napolis Christian Fellowship, a partner church of DCFI. During ICF's transition to a cell-based church, Bill started adult, young adult and youth cells from one original youth group.

Thanks for the valuable contributions of others who helped make this book possible.

Introduction

Today, more than ever before, youth are searching for real, stable relationships that can nurture and encourage them along the way in the often bewildering time of life called *adolescence*. They are hungry for intimacy, community and a sense of belonging.

Often a church will provide youth with lots of meetings and activities. What the youth are looking for, however, is someone who can be a spiritual father or mother to them.

This book tells how youth cell groups can provide informal places for youth to develop close relationships and be trained in ministry. We know it works, because we've experienced it. DOVE Christian Fellowship International (DCFI) is a family of cell-based churches which started in Pennsylvania 20 years ago.[1] Since that time, we have trained believers of all ages to play an active and vital part in the body of Christ by participating in cell groups. This book is written by youth leaders from DCFI and is directed toward helping youth leaders reach youth from junior high age to post high age. (For readers outside the USA, junior high refers to ages 11-14, senior high to ages 15-18, and post high to ages 19 and up.)

Use the stories, ideas and tips in this book to help your youth utilize their talents and enthusiasm within a relationship-oriented cell group setting. We believe God is raising up an army of young Christian men and women who will serve the Lord with a passion while living in close relationship with each other.

[1]The full story of DCFI's development of cell group ministry is available in the book, *House to House* by Larry Kreider. See ordering information on page 120.

Differing Perspectives

Technology is changing the world. Picture this: A young executive is stuck in traffic on the way to his office. So, he opens up his laptop computer and checks his email, only to find a request for an order that has not been filled. After dictating e-mails for his supplier and customer into his laptop, his email is sent by cell phone, and the problem is resolved.

As he continues to wait in traffic, he establishes a video link with an associate in another city and holds a video conference to solve yet another problem. Soon traffic begins to move, and the executive later arrives at his office wondering why he even goes there.

Then I thought of my own six-year-old son who will never know some of the things I grew up with. He, in kindergarten, is already learning how to use a computer. The only appreciation he will ever have of a manual typewriter like the one I used in college will be in a history book. It will be to him like my perception of a hand-crank phonograph—something ancient I saw only in old movies. My son will have different perspectives because his life experiences are different.

CHAPTER 1
Today's Youth Culture
(All Alone On the Web)

This generation of teens, often called the Nexters (children of the Gen Xers) is being shaped by an age of post-modernist thought. To fully realize its effects, let's define post-modernism. Modernism is the philosophy which says that contemporary man has the ability to solve the problems in the world. This pattern of thinking breeds hope in people because they expect that, in spite of the problems they see, the world is going to improve. Thirty years ago, there was still a strong belief in modernism. Secular humanism was prevalent and man had been to the moon. There was a heady feeling that with a little fine tuning, the world was going to be a better place.

This is stated so well in a scene from the movie *Apollo 13*. One of the astronauts is in his backyard looking up at the moon with his wife. He says, "From now on we live in a world where man has walked on the moon. It's not a miracle; we just decided to go!" implying that they could do anything they wanted to do. Of course later in the movie, the astronauts almost die in an accident in outer space. In a classic bit of irony, another scene at the end of the movie shows crowds of people praying for the astronaut's safe return!

Modernism didn't solve the world's problems. So the sons and daughters of the generation that thought they had the answers realized, with a grim fatalism that they were in for a rough ride. Post-modernism comes after a belief in modernism. Along with their parents, this millennial Nexter generation sees life as continually spiraling downward. It leaves them without hope, searching for purpose, sometimes cynical and pursuing self-centered, live-for-the-moment life-styles. This generation does not prize living consistently, but picks and chooses life-styles in a way that no generation has before.

To reach today's teens, we must understand what they face and the unique challenges of their generation. Let's look at some of these challenges.

High-tech, low-touch

Another name we could call this generation is an "e-generation" with the "e" being representative of the electronic—e-commerce and e-nature. They are ambitious and independent, spending much of their time in an adult-free world of the Web and video games.

It is the first generation growing up in a high tech society consisting of fast-changing electronic technology. Today's teens are a computer-generated, video-game-playing, TV-watching, compact-disc-listening, e-mailing, fax-sending, cell-phoning generation of kids impatient to get on with life.

However, electronic gadgetry has a dark side. Hundreds of cable television channels include sexually explicit music videos, talk shows and soap-opera-like teen sitcoms bringing dizzying options for entertainment. Professional wrestling heroes as well as Saturday morning cartoons have a menu of violence. Prime time shows and commercials geared to a teenage audience preach easy sex without rules. Video games are no longer just games: they are violent wars on the screen where teens can hunt and shoot down the enemy. The media and latest marketing scheme is shaping our adolescents' desires right in the family room.

The Internet plays a large part in the way this generation lives. Emailing friends next door or in another country can be part of a teen's daily life. Instant messaging allows kids to communicate in concise sound bytes to friends—not just one friend but several at a time, in real time! Researching information on the Web is an important part of the way students complete homework. However, easy access to pornography on the Internet in the privacy of the adolescent's bedroom is a temptation some teens, as well as parents, have not resisted.

The more time spent on the Web, the less time is spent in real face-to-face relationships. Electronics too often provide surrogate parenting in our society because parents are absent, "...placing more value on careers, retirement funds and their love lives than their parental responsibilities," according to a senior editor of *Newsweek* magazine. "Teenagers of any era tend to be extremely sharp and perceptive. They can see what a society values. If the culture around them has higher regard for professional success and drive than parental responsibility, they are going to absorb it and respond to it." [1]

The position kids are put in because of the lack of physical and emotional touch from caring adults has them operating at an emotional deficit, according to a veteran youth worker: "Most child and youth development researchers concur that millenial kids are exposed to more experiences and information once available only to adults—and at the same time are protected less by the adults and communities that surround them. In other words, they've been dealt a double whammy. Many of the essential assets—which create strong foundations upon which they can build their lives—are missing." [2]

Lack of family ties

An extremely busy family life affords little time to sit around the table and talk after mealtime or spend leisure time together. Teens often follow suit and, like their adult counterparts, plan activities for every hour of the day, even if it is just spending time with peers.

As the traditional, nuclear family disappears, many from this generation are forced to deal with the fallout of their parents' choices. Youth have survived the pain of separation and divorce, with some experiencing multiple breakups. They know the challenges of having mom and dad living in a different part of town or even region of the country. They have gone through a blending of families as parents remarry or take live-in lovers. The high rate of divorce has led young people, overall, to approach marriage more cautiously.

Lack of adequate parental guidance leaves kids disconnected and insecure with unmet emotional needs. Kids are left to find their way through adolescence and its time of questioning by themselves.

Tim Sinclair, a youth leader, noticed that Jeremy, one of the guys in the youth group, was always stopping by his house after school. Jeremy knew the Sinclair family would be home while his own mom and step-dad were still at work. When the younger Sinclair kids got home from school, Jeremy would help them with their homework or just hang out with no motivation to return to his house. The Sinclairs would proceed with dinner preparation, and more likely than not an invitation would be extended for Jeremy to join them. He never refused. The Sinclairs soon realized that he just loved being a part of their family. He enjoyed and needed the sense of security he experienced there. Like many of today's young people, he desperately needed to feel connected in relationships with some sense of emotional security.

Success is too often defined in material terms

Teens today, growing up in a materialistic society, expect to have even better life-styles than their parents. In the United States, material provision has not been a problem for many kids. They have grown up in a time of relative peace and during an era of booming prosperity and the longest economic expansion in U.S. history with the stock market recording new highs. They have had all their physical needs met (and most of their desires). Well-meaning parents perpetuate the impression that the pursuit of money and subsequent material gain leads to success in life. They push their children to project successful, smart, and beautiful images.

An American missionary serving in a Buddhist country was surprised to discover that her host country's youth were as materialistic and pleasure-seeking as her home country's youth. The gods of this generation's youth are the same in many cultures—materialism and pleasure.

Parents sometimes see their kids as status objects that bring value and worth in the eyes of other adults. Achieving fame and public recognition is encouraged. It is little wonder that the mental health of teens today is disturbed by eating disorders, sleep problems, rising obesity, and substance abuse. The pressures they face to be successful (get a good education, job, house, car) are enormous.

Yet physical and material provision is not enough to help kids build healthy and whole lives. They mature physically but are emotionally underdeveloped as families suffer from disconnected relationships with an abundance of choices.

Peer pressure

Because this generation is isolated from adults and more independent, they are exceptionally peer-driven. As kids look for their own values and experience the normal breaking away from the authority of their parents, they often find comfort in numbers. They are a team-playing generation that plays soccer together and wants to belong.

Another reason they tend to be more team-oriented may be due to the networking technologies of today's world and the encouragement in schools to work in groups. This is a good thing. It actually helps young people to feel connected and affirmed in relationships.

Yet too often, the peer pressure is great. Many times, there is no one at home to say "no" when kids experiment with sex, drugs and alcohol in an attempt to fit in. A full-page ad, taken by The Office of National Drug Control Policy in a major U.S. magazine, sent out this plea to parents to keep their kids from experimenting with drugs with the headline, "Parents: the antidrug." It showed an innocent looking young girl asking her parents to "stay involved in my life."

Adolescents need adults in their lives whom they can trust and who earn the right to be involved in their lives. Young people need love and physical affection which develops a sense of security for them. Subsequently, if they feel the world is unstable, parental support offers them a refuge to come home to, a place where people truly value and love them. They need parents' undivided attention. However, parents who are distracted by making a living do not give them the quality attention they need and the chance to say how they feel or to talk about their fears.

Get real

Most youth place a high value on being real and open. They love truth, speak truth to each other, share opinions without fear of offending, and can walk away as friends. They want that same kind of honesty and openness from adults. They are not interested in a candy-coated, watered-down truth. They will not tolerate false, fake, or double standards.

Adults need to be themselves as they reach this generation of young people. Kids spot a fake in a minute. C.S. Lewis describes the kind of leader he ascribed to be: "Think of me as a fellow patient in the same hospital who, having arrived a little earlier, can give some advice." Adults do not have all the answers, but they can give guidance to teens if, by their genuine love, they have earned the right to speak into their lives.

An important strength of today's young people is that they are generally willing to work with a person of another color or sex. Unlike previous generations, they accept interracial dating and are comfortable with blending cultures. This generation has no aversion to one of their peers giving birth to a mixed race baby. While there still are pockets of racism within certain groups, most young people today are open to the cross-cultural arena. Technology is bringing diverse people closer together. Openness and understanding of many cultures different from their own gives them a unique advantage.

Young people also enjoy deep discussion. After cell meetings, we've discovered that the kids often stay late sharing "heart issues" and vision. Yes, they do actually have vision!

Spiritual quest

The spiritual profile of this generation is quite complex. Many kids are willing to identify with organized Christianity in church youth groups and organizations like Fellowship of Christian Athletes because the limits these groups set offer an anchor amid decay in families, schools and streets.

Other young people take a different view. "In place of strict adherence to doctrine, many teens embrace a spirit of eclecticism and a suspicion of absolute truths," reveals a 1999 poll of teenagers by religious researcher George Barna. More than half agreed with the statement "all religious faiths teach equally valid truths." [3]

Kids today are more accepting of each other's beliefs and tend to have a religious smorgasbord for their belief system. This pattern of belief accelerates through the Internet as kids are offered an assortment of belief systems in one click. "Here's exposure to pluralism in a way that no generation has had it before," says a professor of religion at the University of California.[4]

Can the postmodern generations be reached? What is the answer to all this pluralism, relativistic thought? How do we reach today's youth culture?

The new debate about truth

Thanks to postmodern thought, the debate is no longer about what the truth is. The question has become "Does truth exist?" Yet, to say there is no truth is self-contradictory. The statement, "It is true that nothing is true" is nonsense because it is an absolute statement.

Saying that truth is whatever an individual chooses it to be for himself does not work in the real world. The world created by an LSD experience says that one can fly. However, jumping from the tenth floor window will prove fatal, every time! In countless ways, we show that we know the meaning of truth: the plane either crashed or it didn't.

The biblical world view

The biblical world view explains human life adequately and enables us to live a fulfilling life according to its teaching about our place in the scheme of things.

Modern man finds himself adrift in ideas. It has become clear that reason, science and technology have not solved all of our problems. Poverty, crime, and despair defy our attempts at social engineering. The most thorough attempt to restructure society according to a rationalistic, materialistic theory was communism, and it fell to pieces. The collapse of communism was the beginning of the end for modernism. Marxist evolution simply provided no rationale for respecting human dignity.

The dignity of the individual is biblically based. From the biblical revelation, the Western world gained the understanding of man as created in the image of God. Reverence for life, the sanctity of the family, the rule of law, and the idea of right over might (tyranny) all come from the Bible's influence over Western culture.

Postmodernism has exposed the problems of modernism, but it offers no solutions to these problems. Modernism was a dead-end, but postmodernism is chaos. Postmodernism is a formalized anarchy under which none can live for long.

Our modern prophets

Artists and writers often show a prophetic sensitivity to social trends and values before the population as a whole is aware of them. They are sometimes intuitively brilliant people who perceive the end result of a world view long before everyone else. What does modern and postmodern art say? It is often despondent, chaotic and without hope. Francis Schaffer argued that contemporary artists and writers clearly show the modern secular world view is depressing and destructive to man.

Does the New Age offer answers?

There is evidence of real supernatural manifestations in New Age experiences. What these supernatural experiences imply is determined by a person's world view. Do the memories of past lives prove that a person had a past life? Or does it imply demonic communication which is mistaken for memory?

Does reincarnation really explain injustices in the world as the result of judgments from past lives (karma)? The caste system in India is an example of a society in the grip of reincarnation belief; it is oppressive beyond anything in Western society. Don't interfere with the workings of karma, we are told. Leave the destitute in their state.

The biblical concepts of corporate judgment from generation to generation seem much more powerful as explanations of inequality among nations, people groups and individuals. The power of the gospel breaks the cycles of inherited sickness, poverty and sin. How can a New Age philosophy, that offers as its best hope for peace the absence of conflict between nations, compare with a Kingdom that promises a lion and a lamb will lie down beside each other?

Why are we intimidated by these world views anyway?

Since communism fell, and the theory of evolution is at the heart of communism, could that mean that the theory of evolution will also fall in the coming years? Secular humanism and modernism have passed, but the arrival of postmodernism has brought no viable answers. New Age spirituality only brings confusion with it. The very distinctives that separate Christianity from these failed world views must now be boldly proclaimed and explained.

The church cannot compromise its message to attempt to appeal to society as it has historically done. Christians should take advantage of the death of modernism to confess the historical biblical faith to a lost and confused generation. The church can't succumb to the spirit of the age or be intimidated by it. We must boldly contrast the faith and hope of the biblical world view with postmoderism chaos. To be an influence in the postmodern era, we must simply proclaim the truth of God's Word, the validity of God's law, and the eternal sufficiency of the gospel of Christ.

Teens today have a desperate need for basic securities and truth to help them cope with the options in the world.

In conclusion

Raised by television and computers, the postmodern generations are connected with diverse world views and thoughts. The essence of post-modernity is that young people do not feel they have to live consistently, but can "pick and mix life-styles," according to Laurence Singlehurst, director of *Youth With A Mission* England. Nevertheless, teens today have a desperate need for basic securities and truth to help them cope with the options in the world.

"The church needs to move with the changing world," says Singlehurst: "The past 20 years have seen, for the first time in history, the emergence of a worldwide youth culture. Youth in Delhi listen to the same music and follow the same fashions as youth in London, New York, or Rio: they are all being influenced by the same postmodern trends. The Western young person is heavily influenced by the concept that there is no truth to live by...It is only about what I experience and believe...All over the world, young people are beginning to have a similar framework and set of cultures." [5]

These postmodern youth, scattered across the world, desperately need absolute truth to live by. Along with the truth of God's Word that never changes and gives them hope, they have a need for real, devoted relationships they can depend on. Secure relationships will help steer them in the right direction and provide them with an environment conducive to utilizing their talents and enthusiasm.

Youth cells can help provide these relationships. In the next chapters, we will help to make this connection for you.

Helpful Resources for Understanding Youth

Walt Mueller, *Understanding Today's Youth Culture,* (Wheaton, Illinois: Tyndale House Publishers, Inc., 1994).

Daniel Juster, *The Biblical World View,* (Bethesda, MD: Austin & Winfield Publishing, 1995).

Notes

[1] John Leland,<newsweek.com> May 5, 2000, p.4.

[2] Saleem Ghubril, *Youthworker,* November/December 1999, p. 38.

[3] Gene Edward Veith, Jr., *Postmodern Times: A Christian Guide to Contemporary Thought and Culture,* (Wheaton, IL: Crossway Books, 1994).

[4] John Leland, "Searching For a Holy Spirit," *Newsweek*, May 8, 2000, p. 63.

[5] Laurence Singlehurst, "Youth Cells Growing All Over the World," *Advance*, April-June 2000, p. 8.

CHAPTER 2
Youth Cell Groups—
Christian Community
at Its Best

This generation of high-tech young people is deficient of consistent, accountable relationships. Without face-to-face real-life relationships, they remain disconnected relationally, unequipped to face life and its challenges.

Deep inside they long for secure relationships. Today's young people desire affirmation that their thoughts and feelings are valid. They look for this in relationships that are real.

The apostle Paul spoke with an intense longing for relationships in his letters, "...having been bereft of you for a short while...[we] were all the more eager with great desire to see your face" (I Thessalonians 2:17). He also encouraged churches to "Be devoted to one another in brotherly love" (Romans 12:10).

As the church, we need to be attuned to the needs and hear the cries of young people. We can help direct them along their spiritual journeys. How can this happen? We can provide a place for them to hang out and be themselves in small groups. The informal setting offers them a safe haven where they can participate, airing their feelings and concerns with their peers.

A small group will enhance a young person's ministry to the world as he discovers his own revelation of God. In youth cell groups, young people will learn how to connect with God, with each other and with their world. They learn to live in Christian community that encourages teamwork, accountability, spiritual growth and affirmation of each member.

Here's a working example taken directly from our church's adventure into youth cells...

Our History

DOVE Christian Fellowship International is a group of cell-based churches birthed out of a youth revival. From the start of this first church, youth ministry was extremely important to its founders. A strong ministry of evangelizing and discipling young people ensued. The youth leaders in this young church came from those who had become Christians or were touched by God in the youth revival.

Brian was one of these individuals. Although he himself was young, his leaders believed in him and were affirming of his ability to hear from God. They took time to encourage and honor Brian as he reached out to the church's youth, allowing him to dive head-first into youth ministry.

He recalls, "Our early days of youth ministry training consisted of seeking the Lord for direction and going to conferences held by national youth ministries. We looked for some practical ideas of what we were supposed to be doing. As young leaders, without formal training for ministry (my degree in industrial engineering was not very useful in leading young people!), our tendency was to glean ideas from other groups and organizations."

Along the way, by trial and error, we learned many lessons. In the remaining pages of this chapter, we will share with you what we initially learned about youth cell ministry and its benefits.

Our youth group failures

Although we picked up many valuable insights at these confer- ences, we ended up implementing things in youth ministry just be- cause we saw others doing them successfully. However, we only experienced limited success with these ideas. For some reason, it seemed like things that worked for other ministries did not work for us, probably because we were copying their methods without really understanding the *values* behind the methods. Even when the values are understood, there is still the question of, "Is this what God is telling *us* to do with our group *right now*?"

Finally, after seeing the latest program we got from somebody else fizzle out, the youth leaders and church leadership began to seek the Lord for whatever it was we were missing.

Our youth cell idea

Then it dawned on us. Youth could have their own cell groups! DOVE had been cell-based since it began in 1980. It started out in relationship-oriented home cell group meetings during the week and clusters of cells coming together for Sunday celebrations similar to the early church as described in Acts 2:46-47: "Every day they continued to meet together *in the temple* courts. They broke bread *in their homes* and ate together with glad and sincere hearts, praising God and enjoying the favor of all the people. And the Lord added to their number daily those who were being saved."

This dual emphasis on the home meetings and public meetings is reinforced in Acts 20:20: "You know that I have not hesitated to preach anything that would be helpful to you but have taught you *publicly* and from *house to house.*"

> In youth cell groups, young people will learn how to connect with God, with each other and with their world.

Why couldn't the youth benefit from this dual emphasis? Cell ministry was inbred in the genes of DOVE young people from the beginning. Most of the youth attended cell groups with their parents. Still, with only a few exceptions, young people were not the focus of the cell groups. They often ended up sitting in cell meetings, staring at their sneakers in boredom, going out to play basketball, or taking care of the children during the cell meeting. In fact, one of the questions that was raised when youth cells were proposed was, "Who will do the children's ministry?" In other words, the youth were not receiving ministry, nor were they the focus of ministry in the existing family oriented cell groups.

In spite of DOVE's history, the idea of youth cells was new and seemed radical. There were some youth in our group who were new Christians and did not come from Christian families. After much discussion and prayer with our leadership, we decided to start a youth cell with some of the youth who came from non-Christian homes.

At about this same time, some parents felt that their children were being left on the sidelines in a family cell group and asked for a new cell to be started with youth as the focus.

These two cells began to meet in homes weekly. While we started the new adventure of youth cells, we continued to have weekly youth group activities.

Our experiment worked!

We found these two experimental cells to be overwhelmingly successful. The youth loved them. The youth had close discipleship relationships in their cell and also continued to have the larger youth group to attend, mirroring the same strengths the adult ministry was experiencing.

Youth cell groups became an informal, casual place youth could take their friends. We were careful not to imply that these youth cells were better than the adult/family cells. As they expanded, we did not require the youth to attend youth cells. They were given the freedom to go with their parents to the family cell or get involved in a youth cell, whatever met their needs best. We felt it was important that the youth felt affirmed and not forced into one pattern. Eventually, however, most of the youth got involved in the youth cells, along with some of their friends who got saved. A cell group of peers was just too exciting to pass up!

This was the start of youth cell ministry at DOVE. These first cells multiplied into others as leaders were raised up, reproduced mostly from within. By following this pattern, all the new cell leaders had the chance to actually experience youth cell ministry before becoming leaders.

A word of caution

Please, please, please do not take this youth cell information as a pattern and start to implement it at your youth group without understanding the values behind it. Ask the question, "Why are we doing what we are doing?" Do we value and believe the church should be built on relationship and trust, releasing the youth to do the work of ministry? This change in vision and values must take place before you start youth cell ministry.

In addition, remember that the way you implement these new values in youth cells could look different from our model. You do not have to be a carbon-copy of another model in order to build successful cells. Glean what you can from this book, but make sure you adapt it to fit your unique needs as you follow the leading of the Holy Spirit.

God's design for youth cells

Very simply, youth cells are God's design to provide the following for youth:
1. An environment of security and "family."
2. Help to grow in the "character-cooker" of cell life.
3. The challenge to have a live, up-to-date relationship with Christ.
4. Leadership opportunities.
5. Encouragement in reaching their friends and the lost.
6. A connection between the younger and older.
7. An opportunity to accept the responsibility of being Christians at their own level.

What cells should look like

A youth cell is a place where a youth leader is a spiritual parent to one or two teens (these teens may serve as assistants in the cell group). The leader encourages and protects the teens, while helping them to reach out to their peers. As these teens spiritually parent other youth in the group, spiritual and numerical growth occurs in this small Christian community. Eventually the original teens-in-training can lead the group or new groups.

A cell group should be small in its numbers or it will not accomplish its purpose of close relationships and giving everyone a chance to be involved. The youth can recognize that it's not "like it used to be" when numbers swell. When a cell group gets too large, not everyone can share, and it's harder to talk about personal issues. About 12 people is the maximum number for successful interaction.

A cell meeting can include some worship, a short teaching, prayer time and fellowship afterward. The cell group is not simply a Bible study or a mini-church service, even though some great teaching and worship may happen. The cell leadership should lead the meeting but many of the members can be involved. Youth can be encouraged to step out and pray or teach a lesson for the first time. Youth cells need to be informal places with times to talk, process life and the Word of God together.

A simple snack can help to build fellowship, but it is not essential. The youth and/or parents can help provide it. The food can be a benefit but should not be a burden.

Youth meetings and cells work hand in hand

In a small church, you may have only enough youth to comprise one cell at first. As the group grows and multiplies, a youth celebration meeting where all the youth cells come together can also be implemented.

In the cell groups, the youth can better build relationships with each other. A tangible accountability results from these close-knit relationships. Although the larger youth celebration meeting accomplishes some of the same goals of the cell group, such as good worship and teaching, the cell groups always have the advantage. With their smaller, warm, accepting environment for the youth, close relationships can be formed. Discipleship partnerships can be established and more opportunities to develop ministry skills are available.

Essential outward focus

Although fellowship is an important element to the youth cells, the heart of the cells is discipleship and outreach, just like their adult/ family cell counterparts. Youth cells emphasize knowing God, hearing His voice and walking in obedience. Young people are encouraged to actively participate in the Great Commission by making God known to others since their life-style comes from a personal relationship with Jesus Christ.

When youth cell members get a vision beyond themselves, they will not only work at building relationships with each other, but will additionally begin to have God's heart for others and reach out to evangelize and disciple others. This keeps them from becoming self-focused and stagnant.

Each cell needs to be encouraged to have a purpose or vision. Some youth cells may have a vision for a drama team to present the gospel. Other youth cells may have a vision to work for the community in service projects. Some cells have a ministry of intercession, praying for their unsaved friends or family.

Still others may feel led to reach out to children in the neighborhood, playing games and presenting Bible lessons to them. One cell in Pennsylvania does this by helping with a kid's outreach every week and meeting as a cell group every other week.

Having a common purpose builds unity and oneness among the cell members and gives greater strength to the cell. Outward focus is necessary to avoid becoming ingrown or self-centered.

In fact, cell ministry must be for the purpose of outreach and numerical growth. Acts 2:47 says, "The Lord added to the group daily." Spiritual growth will happen along the way as cell members purpose to fulfill the Great Commission.

Youth cell groups can duplicate the sense of community that the early church experienced as described in Acts. If a cell does not have an outward focus, the group becomes ingrown, stagnant, and eventually loses its life.

An illustration to help grasp this concept is to picture four or five people standing in a circle facing each other and holding hands. The group is in unity. But the more time they spend looking at one another, the more they become aware of each other's shortcomings and imperfections and the more exaggerated they become. Also, as they face each other, what is exposed and unprotected? Their backs! They are open for attack from the outside.

Now, picture the same group holding hands but with each person turned facing outwards. Again, the group is in unity. But now the incredible need of the world they are facing dwarfs the imperfections of others in the group. And everyone's back is covered and protected by the rest of the group. Do you get the picture?

Multiplication!

The result of an outward focus is multiplication! The term "cell" itself comes from the multitude of microscopic organisms in the human body that reproduce after their own kind through a process biology calls *mitosis*. A cell by definition is something that grows and reproduces.

In a youth cell, kids are being consistently trained peer-to-peer. As they build Christian community and reach out to their friends, the group grows because leaders are trained from the ground up and new believers are brought in. Before you know it, the group is ready to multiply and start another group.

From the first meetings of a new cell group, the new cell leader must talk about growth and impart vision for multiplication. This clear communication gives a cell healthy direction, so members are not shocked by changes later on.

Cell options

A cell group ministry is unique in that it offers many options for kinds of cells. This creativity and flexibility could express itself in creating youth cell groups that cater to a special interest group. For example, you could create a sports cell for those interested in reaching others through sports, an all girls' or all guys' cell, or a cell with kids from the same school. Some special cells are best designated for a season of time rather than for a permanent basis.

The basics

Whatever model is used, the two essential ingredients are the same—that is, youth cells and a celebration of those cells in a corporate youth meeting. In these two components, the youth mirror what the rest of the church is doing. The creativity comes in the frequency, location, type of cells, leadership and celebration. These vary according to the needs of the group and the vision of the youth leadership and local church leadership.

Youth cells in homes and corporate youth gatherings

The primary method that is used in youth groups is to have the youth cells meet in homes during the week and have a corporate youth gathering at the church facility on a regular basis.

Youth cells in homes. The youth enjoy the natural relationships and community that a home allows. A home provides a relaxed environment where walls can come down. Youth are used to spending time with friends in homes and are encouraged to bring friends. Beware, they will stay late (if curfews allow!). The youth cells in homes meet every week or every other week. This depends on the desire of the youth to get together and the endurance of the leaders! The cells can be either gender-based or coed.

Corporate youth gatherings. The corporate youth meeting is where the cells come together. It can be held every week, but many times will be held every other week or once a month. This meeting is generally at the church facility or youth room, a place where instruments and a sound system can be used as the group size dictates. This youth celebration appears similar to a traditional youth meeting, except the teaching is probably parallel to what is being taught in the cells. Depending on the current emphasis in the youth group, this corporate meeting can take on an evangelistic nature.

Keep hanging in there

Just like seasons we experience on the earth, there are seasons with youth cells and youth ministry. Sometimes the kids in your cell may be ready to take on the whole world. Sometimes they just want a rest from the fight, or they may even have questions about who the enemy really is. A youth leader once said, "When the youth are doing well, don't get too excited, and when they are doing poorly, don't get too depressed either. Just keep praying and focusing on long term results."

We are interested in seeing youth build a foundation for a lifetime of serving and being in relationship with the Lord. Life is a marathon, not a sprint.

It is important not to have huge expectations that place pressure on youth to perform or make them feel like they are failures, unable to measure up to your dreams. Because a cell leader knows the youth in his group well, he or she can focus on each of the kids, helping them to grow. Continue to pray, sharing cell vision.

A Cell Group
All Their Own

I served as an assistant cell leader in an intergenerational cell before launching into youth cell leadership. I was amazed how different it was to be a youth cell group leader. Getting together every other week and having a party once in a while wasn't going to "cut it" with this group. If the relationships were going to be strong and healthy in the youth cell, I knew we needed to step up the intensity to meet the energy level of the youth. In fact, I needed to rearrange my schedule in order to have more time for these young people.

CHAPTER 3
How Relational Youth Ministry Works

One day Shawn received a phone call from a gentleman who wanted to discuss youth ministry. This man had been assigned the task by his church of developing a philosophy for youth ministry, and he wanted Shawn's input as a youth leader. When they met, he immediately asked Shawn a pointed question, "What are the basic philosophies of your youth ministry that you could not be without?"

Shawn recalls, "I looked at him a little funny and then started to ramble. Even as I started to talk, I realized I had not seriously thought about how youth ministry really works. Ministry often is a complex and difficult thing to articulate and develop. But my experience has been that many times we make ministry much harder than it really is."

After rambling a bit, Shawn started to focus on what he really believed. He came to the conclusion that there are three ministry basics that are extremely important in leading youth cells effectively: The leader must have an intimate walk with God, a leader must allow God to change each member, and the group should have specific purpose and goals—including prayer, evangelism and discipleship.

Are you alive?

The first basic truth is that, more often than not, ministry comes out of that which God is doing in our own individual lives. A youth cell leader needs to be ministering out of an overflow of his or her personal walk with God. How can we encourage, train and see others grow in their relationship with God if we are not having a close, intimate walk with God in our own lives?

When flying on an airplane with children, we are told in the event of an emergency to first secure our own oxygen mask before attending to the child's mask. With our own mask in place, we will then be alive to save the child! The same is true in ministry. As a more mature leader, our personal time in prayer and meditation with God is vitally important (it keeps us alive) so that we can effectively lead younger Christians to mature faith in Christ.

Most groups ultimately take on some of the characteristics of their leader. The things that are important to the leader eventually become important to the group they are leading. This is true in many settings such as businesses, organizations, and even the church. We, as leaders, need to first check our own lives and make sure that we are not asking people to commit to something that we are not living out ourselves. We must first be convinced that what we are teaching is truth before we ask others to base their lives upon it.

Additionally, we must walk humbly. Why do we often place "ministry," and especially full-time ministry, at a high and lofty place? *All* Christians are called to ministry, including youth. Each has a calling and obligation to minister to others every chance they get. Those of us "in the ministry" are called by God to train, encourage and equip others to minister. We serve, administer, and coordinate activities to accomplish that goal. But we are all ministers together. Ministry is really quite simple when we have a proper perspective of what it is.

Youth leaders can't change youth

It is only the Lord who can change a heart. Youth leaders can promote fantastic cell groups and activities for kids but the kids must develop their own strong faith so they can handle all the world is throwing at them. If spiritual growth is to happen, it must start to sprout deep in an individual's heart.

Youth leaders at our church learned early on that irregardless of their best efforts, it is always God who changes individuals' hearts. Youth leader, Sarah, became frustrated as she led a group of kids—good kids—but without a real desire to serve God. So she and the other leaders began praying. And they prayed and prayed and prayed.

Then on a weekend retreat, Sarah and the other leaders saw God invade the kids' lives in a way that changed them forever. The kids began to actively seek ways to get to know and serve God better. Sarah could not in her own strength change them, but in one giant fell swoop, God supernaturally changed their hearts. He used Sarah and the other leaders, but He did the changing.

Brian also remembers going on youth retreats and striving to see the youth change and respond to God. He would come home from these events feeling drained and exhausted. He admits, "I was too consumed with "changing" the youth to even worship God during the worship times. A couple of days were needed to recover from the weekend. And worse yet, there didn't seem to be any lasting change in the youth."

Then Brian crossed over. He went from striving to flowing. His whole philosophy of youth ministry changed. Realizing that he was a co-laborer with Christ, he began to let Him do the work. Any lasting change in the hearts of youth would be because God did it. All of a sudden, the pressure was off of Brian.

The leaders would get the kids who made commitments to the Lord on the youth retreats to give their testimonies about how God had changed them. But within a few weeks or months they would be back in the doldrums of lukewarm Christianity. Something was missing.

Brian found that his striving and emotional pleas brought short term, soulish responses from the youth. They opened their hearts because they liked him and wanted to please him. They even came to the front of the youth meetings and cried and felt bad for the things they had done. But Brian realized he wasn't teaching them to know God.

When God supernaturally changed the youth on the retreat, youth ministry changed from a burden to a joy for Sarah, Brian and the other leaders. It got to be a lot of fun! Now they asked the question, "What did God want to do in the hearts of the youth?"

They could cooperate with God in what He had already started in the kids' hearts. The leaders started to really worship God during the worship times instead of watching the youth and trying to "get them to worship." They came home from youth retreats spiritually and emotionally refreshed because they were now experiencing God intimately themselves.

The youth saw that their leaders really knew God, had a passion for Him, and they wanted what the leaders had. It made them hungry for a close relationship with God themselves. Prayer and worship was no longer a "have to" but a "get to." The leaders had arrived at a new philosophy of youth ministry. Youth leaders do not change youth; God does!

Youth leaders do not change youth; God does!

A purpose and goals

An important ministry basic for youth cells is writing a vision (your purpose) and a mission statement (your goals). Any group needs to have a purpose and some goals to see things accomplished, even a cell-based youth group.

Many times the overall church leadership has already done this, but it's important to do on a youth group level, too, as well as a cell group level. Any type of ministry begins with a vision of what God wants to see accomplished through the group whether it be a home cell group, youth group or church. The vision statement for our family of churches is, "To build a relationship with Jesus and others; and to reach the world from house to house, city to city and nation to nation." Obviously, this can be accomplished practically in many different ways.

A successful youth cell group will develop a vision and write it down. Habbukuk 2:2 encourages us to write the vision down so that it can be proclaimed and those who hear it can run with it. It is a blessing to see a group of people catch a vision and run with it. Not only does it mobilize a group for ministry, but it gives each of them responsibility to be part of their fulfillment of the purposes of God. It allows each member of the cell to be part of something the Lord is doing rather than just receiving from the Lord in a meeting.

Vision and purpose needs to be written and communicated frequently. People in our cells and youth groups must know what purposes we are trying to accomplish. This helps to focus the group's energies, gifts and resources. Persistence pays off.

As ideas for activities come up, we can ask ourselves if the ideas fit or accomplish something within our vision. Or we can place within activities things that teach, reinforce, or encourage principles that help in accomplishing our goals. Youth need time to just "hang out." These are important times of relationship-building. But, you see, even this is accomplishing our goal of discipleship and relationship-building.

For example, in planning a retreat, we decide on a theme. Then we plan activities to connect to that theme while accomplishing our vision as a group. We will plan quiet times. Sessions will focus on issues that relate to the theme and our vision. We will have times for relationship-building. As all these things work together, we see God's purposes accomplished, and the group grows spiritually and in numbers.

A leader needs to ask God to give each individual in his or her care a personal vision for prayer, evangelism and discipleship because they are three things that are essential to youth ministry and vision. They should be important to any youth ministry and encouraged as basic spiritual values on an individual level as well as the youth cell group level.

Prayer challenge

It is important to remember that groups are made up of individuals. Each individual should be covered in prayer daily. This might seem like an impossible goal with large groups, but it is another situation where cell groups help.

In the cell group, it is the cell leader who needs to take responsibility to see that each person in his or her group is prayed for daily. Others in the group can help, but the leader is responsible to see it happen. A person who oversees the cell group will pray for the leader of the cell, and cell members are encouraged to pray for their leader. In this way, the whole group is wrapped up in prayer. Assistants may cover two or three individuals.

Prayer is communication with God. Communication is a two way street. Prayer is not only petitioning the Lord for our personal requests. It is also listening to God and obeying what He tells us to do. Youth crave a real relationship with God and can have it, if they are willing to pay the price.

Prayer begins with a desire to have God mold our lives into His likeness on a personal level. This happens best during a daily personal "quiet time" with God. When someone makes a commitment to Christ, part of the initial discipleship process is to show him or her, in a practical way, the importance of cultivating a personal relationship with God.

Even teens claiming to be Christians may not have a strong desire for prayer and personal study of the Word. They may never have placed much value on it, or as Revelation 2:4 says, they lost their "first love" for Christ.

In this situation, a leader has to stand in the gap for the youth to return to their first love. Youth leader Shawn, says, "When I found myself struggling with a group of youth lacking in their desire to move on in their relationship with God, I got on my knees, and God came through."

When we begin to pray, we have to be ready for an answer! If we want to see the things of God developed in the lives of the youth, a leader must allow God to develop them in his or her life.

As young people develop a personal prayer life, a leader will find group prayer becomes much easier. It is important to plan regular times of prayer as a large group. Take time to worship and pray. Prayer and worship go hand in hand. Youth enjoy allowing the Holy Spirit to lead them in extended times of prayer.

As the youth learn how to pray, the leaders's load will become lighter as they become more comfortable praying in a group and understand its importance. Do not be afraid of extended times of silence. Many times God is using this time to speak to individuals. In this fast-paced society, a time of silence is healthy. Don't be tempted to quickly end quiet times with a song or someone sharing something to fill the "dead space." Youth are not intimidated by quiet, meditative times. They actually enjoy them and usually hear from God during them. Hearing from God personally is life-changing.

Many times, people who would never pray in a large group will feel more comfortable in a smaller group. Cell groups can provide a place to begin. As they feel more comfortable in this group, they will gain confidence to lead out in larger groups.

Evangelism focus

There are times when the least likely cell is able to lead youth to the Lord each month when other, more "socially acceptable" cells are unsuccessful. Why? They are inviting friends to come to cell! If you don't bring friends, no one comes to the Lord, no matter how popular you might be. So, the first step in evangelism is to invite friends to your cell group!

Every Christian needs to be involved in personal evangelism and outreach. It is part of the Great Commission. Jesus commanded us to go into all the world and preach the gospel. Youth are certainly not exempt. In fact, youth find themselves in a large mission field— school and the teenage peer group.

"As a teen," one youth leader recalls, "I was taught in my youth cell that I was not in school just to learn, but God wanted me to be a light for Him. When God gave me the vision to see my school as a mission field, it changed my outlook on the people I knew there." If youth can capture a vision for evangelism and outreach at a young age, it will revolutionize the rest of their lives and the lives of the people they know.

Cell groups provide a great, nonthreatening environment into which youth can invite their school and neighbor friends. Many youth cell groups meet in homes, and this adds to the friendly family atmosphere. Youth cells are dynamic vehicles for evangelism— empowering teens to reach out to their friends, and providing a place to take them to receive nurture.

Youth in cells are not only encouraged to invite and reach out to their friends, but they are also encouraged to have a group vision for outreach and evangelism. This keeps the cell vibrant and fresh as new people come in and the cell grows. Most people are not gifted in evangelism, but there are many simple things that a cell group can do together that are very effective in opening up opportunities for evangelism (see *Outreach Ideas* on p.94).

Discipleship relationships

Evangelism by itself is not enough. Those who make commitments to Christ need to develop in their relationship with God. Even those who have been Christians for a long time need people around them who can help them grow. We are always personally learning and growing spiritually.

Relationships within the cell provide the perfect place for mentoring to happen. Discipleship is learning how to practically live out godly principles. It is sharing with others what you have learned through personal experience. One youth cell leader of an all girls' cell said, "My cell has grown together into a sisterhood-like bond. We are able to have strong conversations about the Word and what is going on in our lives. The Lord is definitely working." This type of relational response in cell groups is the fruit we pray for!

Relationship is the thread that binds us to God and to others. Each of us has a need and desire for meaningful relationships. As Christians, we need to develop relationships with those who have similar vision and purpose. In effect, we are discipling each other simply by relationship.

Much of what we say and do affects those around us. Herein lies an important, fundamental basic for youth cells: they are most effective when active and healthy relationships are present. Cell-based ministry can become just a nice program if relationships are not being built. Jesus gave us the perfect model of discipleship—active relationship with practical application of truths and ministry.

Three major areas of relationship for youth include a relationship with God, parents, and peers. They are intertwined, so when one area is affected in a positive or negative way, the other areas are affected in the same manner. For instance, if a youth becomes involved in a group of peers that has a negative influence on him, his relationship with God and his parents are affected in a negative way as well.

Youth want relationship with God

Each youth must have a desire and vision to cultivate a relationship with God for himself. This must hold top priority. All other relationships must stem from this one. When it is healthy and vibrant, the other areas will follow accordingly.

Proverbs 29:18 states, "Where there is no revelation, the people cast off restraint; but blessed is he who keeps the law." This word *revelation* means prophetic *vision*. So without a vision from God or a revelation of God, there will be no restraint. We approached this all wrong in the past. We told youth to have restraint (don't do these things) and we thought that a relationship with God would follow. However, the Bible says the exact opposite.

Simply stated, the best deterrent to sin for a teenager is *vision*, not *rules*. A list of do's and don'ts has no power to keep a young person from all the distractions and snares of this age. In fact, Paul wrote to the Christians in Rome telling them that the law actually stimulates sin. Romans 7:8,10 records Paul's words, "But sin, seizing the opportunity afforded by the commandment, produced in me every kind of covetous desire. For apart from law, sin is dead...I found that the very commandment that was intended to bring life actually brought death."

Instead, the youth need to know that God loves them and has a purpose for their lives. They need to hear that they are God's work-manship created in Christ Jesus to do good works, which God prepared in advance for them to do. They need to know that God wants to know them personally and intimately.

In I Samuel 25, when Abigail appealed to David to not punish her foolish husband, listen to what she said: "When the Lord has done for my master every good thing he promised concerning him and has appointed him leader over Israel, my master will not have on his conscience the staggering burden of needless bloodshed of having avenged himself." It worked! Abigail reminded David that he was called to be King of Israel. It saved him from something that could have short-circuited that call. The restraint a young person needs to obey God's Word will come from his relationship with God and an awareness of God's call on his life. If there is no revelation, there will be no restraint.

This relationship is cultivated through personal quiet time with God. Prayer, studying the Word and worship all play a vital part. Within the youth cell setting, a leader can offer creative quiet time ideas and practice them right there in the meeting (see "Time With God," p. 112). Once youth get a taste of God and His love, they will hunger for more.

A leader's relationship with God will be one of his/her greatest tools in developing hunger in the youth's lives. This is a challenge and will, in turn, challenge the cell groups. There are many things vying for our attention and pulling us away from our personal time with the Lord. But we must make a decision to give this relationship top priority in our lives. We want to minister to youth out of an overflow of what God is doing in our personal lives. Even the success of large numbers of youth will pale in comparison to what God will do with a group of people who have a deep, personal relationship with Him.

Youth want relationship with parents

Youth, although they may not always admit it, have a real desire to be in relationship with their parents. They want their parents' affection, time and attention. Unfortunately many youth today have major breakdowns in this relationship. Sometimes parents push and pressure their kids too much. Kids stress out or begin to feel like failures. This can lead to depression and even suicide.

Other kids battle their parents over rules and restrictions they consider too stringent, like curfews or driving and dating privileges. A youth leader will find himself confronted with a variety of parent-youth conflicts.

Keith Yoder, of *Teaching the Word Ministries,* says youth have the ability to swing from child to adult as they please. When it suits them to be adult, they will hold their own ground and call their own shots. When the going gets tough, they will swing back to the child again, wishing for an adult to show them the way and make the decision. The difficulty for the parent is that, only the young person knows which role he or she is currently preferring!

It is heartbreaking to see the lack of parental relationships for our youth. Teens come home day after day to an empty house. Sometimes parents are missing out of necessity, as in a single parent home where the parent needs to work long hours to make ends meet, but often parents are "missing" where both mom and dad both work so they can give their children anything they ask for. Money does not buy happiness or security for teens.

Unfortunately, this doesn't exclude Christian homes. Youth leaders need to encourage parents to spend time with their children, getting to know them as budding adults, with their own likes and talents. At the same time, parents must give direction and discipline as appropriate. Parents must convey to their children that God's definition of success is different from the world's.

The many parents who have invested countless hours and taken time to listen and learn from their teenagers must be commended. It is heartwarming to see families who have truly healthy relationships. These teenagers seek input and advice from their parents and then respect their authority when they make a decision.

Youth need to love, honor and respect their parents according to Ephesians 5:1-2. Some parents do not have good relationships with their teens and, even those who do, inevitably are going to have conflicts. But, the Word of God stands true. When young people choose to obey the Word of God and respect their parents, they begin to see God changing their hearts.

Youth leaders need to encourage parents as well as teens to dialogue on a reasonable level, without raised voices and uncontrolled emotions. This is a learned skill, developed over time. Many disagreements can be resolved as parents and youth talk heart to heart about their differences. One girl in our youth group felt that her father limited her freedom of hanging out with friends, especially when guys were present. The youth leader encouraged her to ask her father what his concerns were. As they talked together, they were able to come up with a strategy to resolve his concerns while assuaging her feelings of being overcontrolled.

Youth workers can support families by providing seminars and activities that encourage interaction. Suggest a Father-Daughter night out. Provide a parents' information evening allowing for feedback from parents. Be sure to notify parents of upcoming community and church wide events designed for parents of teens.

Youth want relationship with peers

Friends are important to every human being, especially to youth. Acceptance by peers is one of the most important needs in a teen's life. Youth have an overwhelming desire to be valued by others within their age group. According to a survey by Teenage Research Unlimited, a market research firm, peer pressure is at the top of a list of things teens dislike most about being teens.[1] Today the pressure to be "cool" and accepted drives youth to do drugs, drink alcohol, and wear the latest fads.

Teens can better resist the negative peer pressures if they choose their friends wisely and spend time with those who model positive behavior. They should be encouraged to nurture cross-cultural relationships and care for others as they build a clear sense of identity.

There are several categories of relationships that most people have. The first one involves two to three close friendships. These are our "best friend(s)." A second is a group of 12-15 people. These are people that the youth hang out with on weekends. Some call this their "gang or posse." The third is a group of 40-50 people. This group is the sports team, youth group, or the band. The fourth involves a large crowd, hundreds or thousands of people. These groups may be at concerts or football games. People have a desire to be involved in something big, and youth are no exception. Each of these levels of groups are important, but the first two groups could make the difference between a teen who decides to follow Christ and one who does his or her own thing.

Youth cells focus on the first two groups. They are effective because they provide youth with an environment to build close-knit Christian relationships. This is important because in order for youth to grow spiritually, they need people, especially peers, around them to influence and affect them in a positive, godly way.

This does not negate Christian youth from having friends who are pre-Christians. They need to be reaching out to non-Christians, but they need to have Christian relationships in the first two categories to encourage them to grow spiritually.

The following equation, showing the number of relationships within a group, helps you realize why it is so difficult to maintain relationships on a large youth group level. Smaller cell groups bring the number down to a manageable size.

$$r=p(p-1)\div2$$

Number of relationships (r), equals(=), the number of people(p), multiplied by (the number of people minus 1), divided by 2. The following results speak for themselves.

Number of people in a group	Number of relationships within that group
2	1
3	3
4	6
5	10
6	15
10	45
50	1225
100	4950

Each youth is a minister!

Another important concept is that each Christian is called to be a minister. When an individual understands that he or she is a minister, the leader no longer has to carry the burden of doing all the ministry within his group. A leader's responsibility lies in training those within his cell in ministry skills and how to disciple others. By doing this, he reproduces himself.

Notes

[1] "Snapshots," *Youth Worker,* November/December 1999, p. 11.

Creative Growth

My experience as a cell leader began in the family cell in which I was serving as assistant leader. One of the fathers in the cell asked if I would pray about starting something for the youth. Another young adult and I began an exciting journey in which we were both still involved years later. Our band of youth grew and multiplied into two cells each with a school district in focus. The cell I was involved with continued to see new youth joining in, and another cell was multiplied out. This time a post high guy and two senior high girls worked together to provide leadership. Then the cell I was giving leadership to saw several transitions, so we joined with another cell. Later I began a new cell with the focus on junior highers.

Several of my cell leaders were actually quite young. One of the girls was only 12 years old when I asked her to serve as an assistant. With their parents' blessing, these youth contributed greatly to the cells. While many of the kids were involved in teaching and giving suggestions for activities, allowing my young assistants to lead the group really gave them practical hands-on training.

I know of a family cell which creatively met the needs of the youth in their group. An adult planned a teaching just for the youth, and the youth held their own cell in another part of the house where the parents were meeting.

CHAPTER 4
Modeling Leadership:
"Show Me; Don't Tell Me"

S itting at the breakfast table in a local restaurant with a young youth cell leader one day, Antonio, a youth pastor, suddenly noticed how obvious he was about peering into his pocket calendar to check the list of things he wanted to talk to the cell leader about. Consequently, the Holy Spirit began to speak to Antonio. Did the cell leader feel like he was just another check on Antonio's checklist of things to do? Was he conveying the message that he cared about the cell leader as a person? Or did the cell leader think Antonio's only interest in him was for what he could accomplish to enhance Antonio's ministry as a youth pastor?

"Since that time," Antonio acknowledges, "my daily checklist accompanies me very little to the meetings I have with youth cell leaders. I trust the Holy Spirit to bring up the points of discussion that are important in these relational settings."

Now when Antonio is meeting with youth cell leaders, his first questions pertain to how the leaders are doing personally. Because Antonio is truly interested in them, he asks questions about their schooling, job, or family life. Leaders have to be healthy people before they can be healthy leaders. Eventually a youth pastor will get around to the questions like, "How is the cell going? How are the youth in the group doing?"

This mode of questioning actually models for the youth cell leader how they can relate to people in their own cell. Cell-based ministry is based on relationships, and youth are hungry to be in relationships that are genuine and real. Ministry that causes a young person to feel like a number within an impersonal program will cause them to shut down. Good youth leadership will provide the stability and structure that youth need and also the relationship and nurture to see them grow personally.

Youth leaders are recognizing that whatever they do, it must be relational in nature. This is a change from the regimented, program-based model that has been used in the past. It is a return to the biblical pattern of spiritual fathers and mothers.

Take me to your leader!

So what kind of people are qualified to lead youth cells? Youth are generally attracted to anyone who has an open heart, is real, and has a home with open doors. We have had very successful youth cell leaders of all ages—some are parents of youth, others are college age, single, married, and some leaders are youth themselves. God calls people from every age group to lead youth cells.

It is probably a good idea for the youth cell leaders to be at least one level of maturity ahead of the people in their group. For example, senior highers lead junior high cells, and if they have the maturity, their senior high peers. Without this maturity, it can prove to be too much of a burden for a senior higher to lead his peers, even with close spiritual covering by youth leaders. It can be difficult for them to be both leader and friend to their peers. Peers leading peers can be a powerful model, but we must admit that we burned out some promising young leaders by not asking them to assist longer before they led their peers. But, God is redemptive!

Assistant cell leadership in peer cell groups is a great training ground. They can give input into the cell, teach and pray for the people in the cell, but do not have to shoulder the full responsibility of the group. When new, tough issues come up, an older leader can add stability and coach the young leader through proper responses to each challenge.

It's worth the risk

Allowing the youth to lead is a continual growth process with many challenging, but rewarding, developments. Leaders have a tendency to view success from an adult perspective; however, we don't always obtain the expected results as quickly with youth leading. The Lord is interested in character growth, which requires dealing with the positives and the negatives. God uses these trials to develop a generation of future leaders willing to seek and depend upon Him.

It is important to take risks with young leaders. If ministry is never released to developing leaders, they will never learn to take responsibility and hear from God for themselves. Challenges cause rapid spiritual growth in young leaders. Get them to teach, lead prayer, help with water baptisms, plan cell meetings, and even lead the meeting. Be creative in distributing responsibilities. Take into consideration the young leader's gifts and strengths, and give responsibilities in accordance to their God-given talents.

In I Corinthians 12, Paul points out that God has given each different gifts so that the body of Christ can be fitly joined together. God doesn't give best or better gifts, but simply different gifts. It is important to understand each youth's uniqueness within his gift and ability.

There must be close prayer and relationship covering by the cell leader in times of taking these risks. Do not challenge youth to take a step of faith and not be there to help if they get in trouble. Most of the time, they will just need your prayers, a word of encouragement, and a few helpful suggestions.

Expect the best; accept the worst

Youth ministry can be messy, but if young people are not allowed to make mistakes and learn, they will not gain spiritual strength. Proverbs 14:4 says, "Where there are no oxen, the manger is empty, but from the strength of an ox comes an abundant harvest."

It is encouraging to see the willingness of many youth who step forward to lead and grow. Many times we know we can lead discussions better than the youth, communicate ideas better, and so on. While that may be true, if we keep the reins in our hands, we limit the youth. God's ability to teach them lessons at an early age will hopefully help them avoid devastating situations in the future. The youth cell level is a great place where, with supervision and encouragement, you see young men and women learn valuable kingdom lessons that will benefit the whole church body.

Perhaps the best philosophy in youth ministry is to always expect the best, but accept the worst. The general atmosphere of love and acceptance in a youth cell is a safe place for individuals to step out and try new things. Expect youth to do great things, but be there for them if they crash and burn. This is really important.

John was a somewhat spiritually insecure kid of about sixteen. He was well-liked and respected by the other youth in the youth cell and by his friends at school. John would sometimes bring his unsaved friends to youth cell or youth activities.

John's youth cell leader had high hopes for him and envisioned him as a cell leader some day. The cell leader had been encouraging John to grow in his walk with God and in leadership roles. Finally, the leader decided to ask him to do the teaching one night at youth cell.

After his initial "no way" response, the leader persisted in encouraging John that he could and should do a teaching. Eventually John said he would do it. The jubilant leader set a time for John to teach and announced John's debut to the rest of the cell group at the next cell meeting.

As the night approached, the leader checked in with John to make sure he had not forgotten about his commitment. John had heard dozens of cell teachings, and the cell leader assumed John would know what to do.

On the night of the cell meeting, the leader confidently announced that John was going to teach and quickly made some announcements. Then he prayed for John and turned the floor over to him.

John opened his Bible to a scripture, read it, commented that he thought this was a good scripture, closed his Bible and looked back at the leader.

The astonished leader, who had fully expected a ten to fifteen minute teaching, tried to draw more out of John with questions, but John had nothing else to say. And neither did anyone else in the group. Eventually the leader moved on to plan B (what you do when your first idea does not work)!

Expect the best, but accept the worst! And in the midst of it all, provide a loving and accepting environment, where youth are not afraid to stumble and fall! A world-class runner has to start someplace. He has to take those first important steps out of the starting block. With practice, he learns how to run a race effectively and smoothly.

A potential leader—an "average Joe"

Concerns that a lot of youth leaders have about youth cells include:

"Where do I get the leaders for youth cells?"

"I am already short of leaders."

" There is no way we can start youth cells!"

We believe there is a vast, untapped reserve of youth cell leaders in our churches. This group could very well be the key for your youth ministry to prosper and grow. It has been overlooked for hundreds of years by the church. Are you ready for the big secret? The vast, untapped group of leaders in our churches are normal, average Christians!

> In a normal youth group, many people are wallflowers, but in cell-based ministry there is a place for all and the friends of all.

Most of our youth cell leaders are not super-gifted, charismatic, guitar-playing, solo-singing, Billy Graham-preaching, "Ken and Barbie" look-a-likes. They are normal people who originally might not even have enough confidence to think they could help with a youth cell group. They need someone to come alongside of them and encourage them. Paul told Timothy whom he should train, "And the things you have heard me say in the presence of many witnesses entrust to reliable men who will also be qualified to teach others" (II Timothy 2:2).

In a normal youth group, many people are wallflowers, but in cell-based ministry there is a place for all and the friends of all. Success stories, of those whom others might not choose, become very positive contributors to the cell process. A potential youth cell leader does not have to be a person with charisma but a person of character.

Encouragement goes a long way!

How do you find these normal, average people of character in your church? As a youth leader, talk to the people you are accountable to and ask them for suggestions. Do they know of any faithful individuals who are filled with the love of Christ and care deeply for teens? This is the kind of person you could approach to ask, "Would you pray about helping with a youth cell? I think you would do a great job." Be an encourager. Most people need encouragement to step out and develop their gifts. They must believe they can do the job you are asking them to do.

Joseph was a Levite from Cyprus who was such an encourager that the apostles actually changed his name to Barnabas, literally translated as "Son of Encouragement." He came alongside and believed in people that no one else thought were qualified. He reached out to Saul when he was such a "hot" item that no one else would touch him because they didn't trust him with his history of persecuting Christians: "When he came to Jerusalem, he tried to join the disciples, but they were all afraid of him, not believing that he really was a disciple. But *Barnabas took him and brought him to the apostles.* He told them how Saul on his journey had seen the Lord and that the Lord had spoken to him, and how in Damascus he had preached fearlessly in the name of Jesus" (Acts 9:26-27).

Later, Barnabas saw a great need for the new Christians at Antioch to be taught, so he recruited Saul to go along with him to teach: "Then Barnabas went to Tarsus to look for Saul, and when he found him, he brought him to Antioch. So for a whole year Barnabas and Saul met with the church and taught great numbers of people..." (Acts 11:25-26).

Barnabas was an encourager. He later stood and encouraged John Mark when Paul was convinced John Mark was a failure: "Barnabas wanted to take John, also called Mark, with them, but Paul did not think it wise to take him, because he had deserted them in Pamphylia and had not continued with them in the work. They had such a sharp disagreement that they parted company. Barnabas took Mark and sailed for Cyprus, but Paul chose Silas and left, commended by the brothers to the grace of the Lord" (Acts 15:37-40).

Barnabas's encouragement later paid off as Mark proved himself to Paul and wrote the second gospel. A little encouragement goes a long way!

In addition to encouragement, potential youth cell leaders need training. They need an existing leader to take them by the hand, and show them how to lead. If adequate training is not given, discouragement and defeat will quickly follow. Condemnation comes when people are encouraged to lead but are not given the proper training to effectively accomplish the work.

Jesus' method of training

Let's look at Jesus' method of training. Jesus followed a four-step process. First, He *declared* to them the information. Then, He *demonstrated* the task for them to observe. Next, He *directed* them to try it. And last, He *debriefed* them, discussing how it went.

"After this, Jesus traveled about from one town and village to another, proclaiming [He declared] the good news of the kingdom of God. The Twelve were with him and also some women who had been cured of evil spirits and diseases... [He demonstrated]" (Luke 8:1).

"When Jesus had called the Twelve together, he gave them power and authority to drive out all demons and to cure diseases...So they set out and went from village to village, preaching the gospel and healing people everywhere [He directed them to go]" (Luke 9:1, 6).

"When the apostles returned, they reported to Jesus what they had done [He debriefed them]..." (Luke 9:10).

Declare

Jesus proclaimed the kingdom of God to the disciples. He taught them what it was and how it worked. This is the kind of training we usually do the most...the how-to, the information, the training seminar or learning about youth cells from a book like this. Jesus even had question and answer sessions.

Hands-on teacher training. DOVE Christian Fellowship International has a practical training tool available that uses this method to train people to teach in cell groups. It's called a *Teacher Training Course.*[1] A group of four cell leaders, assistants or potential leaders get together for a four and a half hour training session. A video teaching on "How to Teach" is shown to the group. Then the leader teaches a short lesson to the group after which each person studies and prepares to teach this same lesson back to the group in front of a video camera. After evaluation, the process is completed again with a different teaching. It is a great time of relationship-building, practical training and gift-releasing. The improvement from the first teaching to the second is usually dramatic.

But this kind of training is not enough.

Demonstrate

Teens need to see how it works. *Demonstration* is the practical modeling of the kingdom of God. Jesus modeled healing the sick, casting out demons, and raising the dead. The kids you are training as cell leaders have to see you minister. Take them along when you are meeting with a teen after school, or have them join you for prayer before a cell meeting. Have them sit in with you when you visit a cell that is not growing. Ask them for their input. What would they have done differently if they were you? What are their observations?

Direct

Jesus commissioned His disciples to go do it. "Okay, boys, it's your turn to try it." Delegate assignments to the person you are training after they have seen you do it. Start with small things and increase to greater responsibilities. Ask them to pray at the close of a meeting. Another night, ask them to lead a prayer time. Give more and more youth cell responsibility to them. Let them cover the entire meeting, including delegating parts to others. Don't be surprised if good things begin to happen, and you see new giftings in others you never noticed before!

Debrief

Jesus debriefed His disciples after He sent out the twelve and the seventy-two. In the latter case, He had to correct them for over-confidence. This time is so important. Listen to the young people tell you about the "new" successful idea that you have done a dozen times. Help them understand "why" if they have failed. This debriefing time shows that you are interested in them as people, not just as potential leaders to unload some of your responsibility onto.

Leaders are released!

If we are to empower and release young men and women into ministry, we must step aside and give them opportunities which most of us were never given as teens. God is faithful to meet our leadership needs, just as He is faithful to provide a blueprint for each church, since no two have the identical makeup.

Releasing leadership to do what they have been trained to do can be one of the most positive things we can do. Since some of us like nice easy steps to follow, this process of seeing leaders released for youth cells would look like this.

- **PRAY** (prayer really works!)
- **RECRUIT** (ask them to help)
- **ENCOURAGE** (tell them they can do it)
- **TRAIN** (equip them to do it)
- **RELEASE** (let them go and do it)

Remember, training includes your modeling ministry to them, giving them the opportunity to try it in a safe environment, helping them learn from their initial experiences, and releasing them to do it.

We usually have a monthly meeting in a leader's home with all the youth cell leaders. This is an informal, relational group where there is freedom to share successes and failures. Prayer is also a part of these meetings. In some settings, this actually becomes a specialized cell group.

Do all become leaders?

After a youth cell leader is called by God (recruited), he or she goes through a process of encouragement and training before they are released. But do all youth become cell leaders? Not always.

However, we believe many can be assistant leaders even if they do not feel led to lead a cell themselves.

Kinds of assistant leaders

There are three different kinds of assistant cell leaders—future leaders, perpetual leaders, and catalyst leaders.

Future leader assistants are those who will eventually lead new cells that are started. They display strong commitment to the group, have leadership capabilities and desire to move ahead.

Perpetual assistant leaders are those who do not have a very strong leadership gifting but are excellent support people. They will always serve as assistant leaders, even in a new cell. They are significant to cell growth and multiplication, but it is important that they do not feel pressured into leading a cell.

Catalyst assistants are leaders in the cell group who are involved in other areas of ministry. For example, a senior high youth might be leading a junior high cell group as a ministry but be involved in a senior high cell group for his or her own spiritual growth. Potentially he or she could be a catalyst assistant leader in the senior high group. These kinds of leaders lead by influence but would not take responsibility for the planning and strategy of the cell.

Possibly a youth group worship leader who puts a lot of time into leading worship would be in a youth cell as a catalyst, but not have the responsibility to lead it. Catalyst assistant leaders bring life, input and vision into the group but will probably not be involved in the nuts and bolts planning of the cell meeting.

Helpful Resource for Training

[1] *Teacher Training Course* available through *House to House Publications* (See web site: www.dcfi.org).

CHAPTER 5
A Youth Cell Leader's Job Description

A very practical tool for cell ministry is writing a job description. It is helpful for a leader to know exactly what is expected of him or her. The following is a sample we have used for youth cell leaders.

Youth home cell group leaders and assistants' job descriptions

- Spend time developing your relationship with God.

- Pray for the youth in your home group regularly and work with your assistants to see each individual covered in prayer daily.

- Your goal is to see each youth walking with God and in the vision of prayer, evangelism, and discipleship. Encourage each youth to live an accountable life.

- Meet with other leaders in your cell to pray and plan cell meetings and activities.

- Pray to see new leaders released and for your cell to multiply.

- Keep in touch with your pastor/overseer with prayer concerns and growth strategy.

- Complete the home cell leadership training course offered at your church. If you have not completed a basic biblical foundation course, do so.

- Participate in the cell group leaders' meetings at your congregation, taking note of the upcoming dates.

- Prayer and preparation are important! Study your teachings and be ready for the cell meeting. Cell nights need to be varied or they will become boring! Plan ahead! This will keep you from a last minute scramble that may be unproductive.

- Watch and listen for areas of growth needed in the cell members' lives that can be addressed in the cell teachings. If it is not an area you are comfortable teaching, invite a guest speaker. Don't forget to take an offering or give a monetary gift to the speaker.

- Make phone calls to keep in touch with everyone, along with personal visits and chats on Sunday mornings or other times when you cross paths with them.

- Have others in cell help with responsibilities whenever possible. Watch for budding gifts in cell members' lives. Get others to help make phone calls when needed. Occasionally meet at someone else's house to give the regular meeting place a break. You'll allow someone else to practice the gift of hospitality! Always be looking for new leadership.

- Take occasional offerings (not tithes) to build the cell kitty for expenses that come up.

Today youth ministry is more about empowering and activating than it is about running programs and entertaining. Young, emerging leaders can and will take responsibility and follow through with it. A youth cell leader should meet with his assistant(s) on a regular basis. But this interaction needs to be more than just a monthly planning meeting. The most important aspect of this time is relationship-building between the leaders. Pray as well as plan.

A cell leader should regularly ask the assistant leaders what they feel God is saying about the cell. Asking for input not only honors the assistants as leaders but also communicates that the cell leader respects their ability to hear from God. Having this type of communication allows for the assistant cell leaders to feel more responsible for the cell group as a whole. They realize they are not just bystanders, but individuals whose prayers and input are vitally needed for the health of the whole group.

Use any resources provided by your church or the local Christian bookstore. Your pastor may provide teachings. There are lots of helpful youth books, videos and teaching tapes that could help in preparation for cell lessons. Take advantage of someone else's labors. You don't have to reinvent the wheel.

The church is
not a building!
It is people in
relationships,
with a vision
to grow
spiritually and
to challenge
others in their
relationship
with God.

54   *Youth Cells and Youth Ministry*

CHAPTER 6
Healing This Generation's Wounds

I s the blood of Jesus powerful enough to bring healing to this hurting generation filled with stress, loneliness, anger, cynicism, disappointment and feelings of victimization? Do we believe that Jesus, the Counselor, is in us as the Bible states in Isaiah 9:6?

A youth leader must answer in the affirmative to the previous questions. Christ, the anointed One, is in us and actively helping us. God, by definition, is supernatural, and He will give us supernatural insight and power to bring freedom into the lives of youth.

When Sarah started working with youth, she remembers, "I could easily plan a spectacular event. That wasn't enough. I knew I had to learn how to meet needs in their lives if there was to be lasting 'heart' change." She realized early on that if young people are not delivered and set free, how will they be able to lay hands on their friends and pray to see them set free? She needed to learn how to get on their level and treat them as valuable human beings with valid feelings and ideas.

Getting on their level

Young people can tell when you really care about what they are going through. Are you willing to look into the eyes of the youth around you and find out what the secret pain is? Really listening is often hard work. It requires reading between the lines and really hearing what is being communicated. When a young person is sharing, he or she can tell if the listener is on the same emotional "wavelength."

Jesus understands loss, grief, abandonment, rejection, and pain. "He was despised and rejected by men, a man of sorrows, and familiar with suffering..." (Isaiah 53:3). He truly can empathize, and in turn we can rely on His presence within us to reach out, connect and bring healing with authentic compassion in any situation. A youth cell leader does not have to experience the same problems someone from his group is dealing with—he just needs to have a heart of compassion to hear their cries.

Healing in the context of relationships

Healing takes place in the context of relationships, both human and divine. What better place for this to happen than within relationships in a youth cell! For real change to occur in teens' lives, especially in our postmodern world, kids have to experience, hear and see truth before they will believe it. In the small relational setting of cell groups, kids can be given responsibility and encouraged to take responsibility for their lives. They can learn to love God and find healing for their deepest pain.

In cell groups, leaders can regularly take time to sincerely focus on young people as individuals. This caring one-on-one emphasis makes the statement, "You are important." Talk to the teens about the sports team they play on or their latest science project. This is an important first step of communication. It opens the door for sharing at a deeper level. A leader must be approachable and undistracted when talking with teens, even in an informal setting. Sincere concern is a key to open the door for serious ministry times later.

Provide positive feedback like "thanks for sharing that." Help the kids know that what they are feeling is normal, and they are not alone. Keep giving them opportunities to talk and air their feelings. Challenge and encourage their thinking processes. Bad attitudes are sin and need to be treated as such. Be quick to stop the conversation and pray for God's help in a situation the teen is struggling with. Then in your personal intercession time, pray for them specifically. You can help keep a small problem from becoming a big one.

Don't allow yourself to take sides in conflicts with parents or peers. Let the teen know that you are trustworthy. Assure the teen that you won't share personal information as part of the gossip grapevine.

Don't overlook "successful" youth. Just because a kid looks like he has it all together does not mean he does. Every kid craves a good dose of tender, loving care with his or her struggles, big or small. Take the time to read between the lines, and don't be afraid to just come right out and ask pertinent questions.

In healing, there must be an emphasis on community. God has a plan for inner healing and deliverance, which includes the whole body of Christ; not just one youth worker, Bible teacher, friend, or counselor. Even the best professional Christian therapists would readily admit they only aid in the healing process. Ultimately, it is the Lord Himself, using a variety of persons, who brings about the healing.

As we interact with the youth within the cell group community, the oil of the Holy Spirit will bring healing. A frequent practice in our youth cells is to have a "hot seat" (a chair put in the middle of the room where the youth sit as they take turns receiving prayer). The youth cell follows the biblical practice of laying hands on the person in the chair for prayer and ministry. All the youth are encouraged to exercise their spiritual gifts during this time. The grace of God imparted through spiritual gifts edifies the giver and receiver. This can be a real growth time for youth who desire to develop their gifts as well as a healing time for people desiring ministry.

Dealing with minors

For youth cell leaders who will be involved in deeper personal counseling, it is important to remember that we are dealing with minors, not adults. Involve the parents in the healing process if possible. Parents can provide valuable support for their child.

It is important that leaders counsel in public or group settings, avoiding "closed door sessions." It is best to have same-gender counseling. If it is necessary to counsel someone of the opposite sex, it is wise to have a third person present.

Knowing when to get more help

Youth leaders have a huge opportunity in kids' lives to help them through difficult situations. Still, there are times when youth cell leaders may not know how to best help the teen. Pastors can be a great source of wisdom for a youth leader, but sometimes even they will need to make a referral to a professional biblical counselor. In the case where a youth is being abused or may be in danger of hurting himself or others, parents and pastors must be involved or, if necessary, the local crisis organization. Christian support groups may also be a source in helping a teen move toward a positive solution for a problem in his or her life.

There may also be times needed for the biblical practice of freeing people from the oppressive hold of demonic spirits. In situations where you, as a youth leader, are unsure if additional help is needed, it is best to talk to your pastor.

It's been said that youth leaders are like conductors who orchestrate symphonies of people, services and community around their kids. They themselves do not have to be experts, but they can build bridges to others who can help our kids.

Educate yourself

Keep your eyes open for seminars or read articles and books that relate to youth issues. All these can help you develop skills in dealing with tough topics such as suicide and unplanned pregnancy. You should understand the teen world and its culture. You do not have to be an expert, but youth leaders who are knowledgeable about hurting teenagers and what they are going through will be much more useful and compassionate advocates for teens. Working with youth means developing your people-helping skills. Never let your fear of inadequacy stop you from being loving and caring. The end result will be that you will grow and mature as a leader in the body of Christ.

Helpful Youth Counseling Resource

Josh McDowell & Bob Hostetler, *Handbook on Counseling Youth*, (Word Publishing, 1996).

CHAPTER 7
Transitioning to Youth Cells and Church Planting

How do you transition an existing traditional, program-based youth group to a relational, cell-based youth group?

A first key in transitioning must be prayer. All decisions of a Christian must be bathed in prayer. How much more so must church leadership be on their knees as they consider major church structure changes! We must take the time to hear God's heart for direction and timing before stepping into the often turbulent waters of transitioning.

Our goal is to seek the Lord and transition to cells the way He is leading our group to go. We want to please Him, and Him only. In humility, we must continually seek God's wisdom and grace for our people as they adjust to the coming changes. Change is rarely easy. Prayer will not only help make the transition less traumatic, it will bind believers together in unity.

God wants His people to be in unity. We must cooperate with the desire of Jesus' heart and "make every effort to keep the unity of the Spirit through the bond of peace" (Ephesians 4:3). Unity is dear to the heart of God. Praying together will jell a youth leadership team to unity and oneness of vision.

Without unity, there can be no agreement of the new vision and values of youth cell ministry. And the vision and values must be clearly understood. The new values for youth cell ministry in a local church must line up with values identified by the senior pastor and elders. If this does not occur, the youth will end up with a conflicting vision, resulting in church problems.

Though it is not absolutely necessary, it is actually best if the whole church is transitioning to cell groups at the same time, not just the youth group. It will be helpful because the parents will also be getting teaching from the Word and hearing vision for cells at the same time as the youth. This will make it easier for the parents to understand and embrace the vision for their teen's involvement in youth cells. Families together can be part of the fresh, new vision.

The cell-based vision is built on the heart and passion for what God desires—making disciples. It is important for the youth to catch and own the vision of the cell groups and the church for themselves. A religious tradition of arriving at a church building Sunday morning or simply showing up to please their parents will not work in a cell-based structure. The cell vision encourages young men and women to live a life-style of personal evangelism and discipleship.

> **The cell-based vision is built on the heart and passion for what God desires—making disciples.**

Teens can understand the cell-based vision and can be an even more productive part of the church today. Through prayer and impartation, the youth can be challenged to get out of the stands and into the field, joining in the game.

Make time during youth events as well as one-on-one to share vision, encouraging them to become a part of the team. It's not just about joining a cell group, it's about becoming part of the action.

Leadership training

Without the dedication, prayer, work and servant hearts of leaders, nothing takes place of lasting value. In the initial transitioning stages, meeting with your youth leadership is extremely critical. It is important to get to the place where you are speaking with one voice and one mind as a team of leaders. Listening to input from your potential cell leaders is very important during this process. Unity at this stage is another key to success in transitioning.

You must spend time fine-tuning the vision for youth cells. You can glean lots of good ideas from other churches, seminars or materials. Of course, no church can duplicate exactly another church's vision for youth cells. Your vision must be based around the needs and gifts of your group. Take the great tips and structure ideas from others, but filter them through what the Lord is saying to you and your youth leadership.

Getting started

Some of the best leadership training for transitioning to cells can be done in a prototype cell. This kind of model cell group should be made up of those who have already committed to be youth cell leaders and others who are potential leaders. In this clear model, you can train and help your leaders to see what a cell is and how it functions. The model should include an outward focus with evangelistic efforts.

Your youth cells will resemble what you model in the prototype cell. Make the quality of this cell a top priority because it will be reproduced over and over. This clear modeling will help your youth cell leaders keep from returning to old "Bible study" paradigms or drifting back to the way things used to be.

Another important reason we recommend starting with a prototype cell is so that everyone present can see, feel and experience the cell multiplication. As this one cell becomes two, they experience praying about which new group they should be involved with.

Not only do these potential leaders experience the cell multiplication, but everyone else is watching this "new" vision from the outside. So, from the very beginning, the ideas of cells growing, multiplying and reproducing is in the DNA of all your cell leaders' vision. This is a critical building block for future growth. Eventually, one cell becomes two, two become three and four, and the transition is underway.

The shotgun start

A transition with a "shotgun" start may have more challenges. A quick overall start, this strategy involves starting several groups all at the same time and encouraging the youth to join one of them. Prior to the start, of course, several leaders are trained in cell group ministry and values, so the new groups have leaders with which to start.

A downside to this method is that the cell leaders do not get the opportunity to experience cell life firsthand before leading a group. They really have to learn on-the-job with no prior experience. This kind of transitioning also does not provide the model of multiplication like the prototype cell does.

But transitioning all at once is a possible scenario. You must know your people and your unique situation. This kind of transition may work for you.

Church planting

When starting with a new church plant, you generally only have one or two teens. Simply start a cell with the youth you have. This may include teens as well as potential leaders. Invite the few youth who are part of the new church plant as you begin to build this first youth cell.

Encourage the teens to bring friends and do some outreach events to see the youth cell grow. Pray for and recruit more leaders as the cell grows and prepares to multiply. After you have two or three youth cells, start a monthly or bi-weekly youth celebration or activity, and the youth group is on the way.

What if there are no youth or youth leaders at the beginning of the church plant? Pray, pray, pray! Youth ministry is a significant part of any church. Without it, a church body is missing a very important ingredient. Ask God to bring teens and youth leadership your way; then keep your eyes wide open. God loves to answer prayer. Don't artificially set anything up, but be ready when the youth start to come.

CHAPTER 8
Worship:
Helping Youth Connect
With God

This generation has a desire to get in touch with God and each other. They want God to be real to them. They want something that connects, that works, and that becomes a life-style. They are less interested in theology and intellectual arguments and more interested in encountering the supernatural. The old way of thinking taught that if you have the right teaching, you will experience God. The new way of thinking teaches that if you experience God, you will have the right teaching. Subjective experience can become a great introduction to knowing God if it is followed up by objective teaching of the Word.

Youth of this generation enjoy worship because it is real and it is safe. God will never leave or forsake them. He is not going to hurt them or make them feel that they don't measure up. They can be confident to learn the ways of love from God, the expert. He is a God who will be gentle, patient and help them learn at their own pace.

Hubie, a youth worship leader in his forties, compares his generation with today's generation concerning one aspect of worship. He observes, "It seems my own generation of peers always loved praising and worshiping with lots of energy, dancing and shouting. I find that youth today like to do the same, but only at certain times. They do not equate energized activity to mean that the

Holy Spirit showed up. In my generation, whenever it got quiet, someone always felt he had to start another song. Looking back at it now, maybe we were uncomfortable with silence."

Perhaps today's Christian young people, with their high energy environment, recognize their need to be still and hear from God. The consequences of not having quiet times with God in today's stressful world is to be constantly stressed out!

A leader should not use a quiet time during worship to preach or automatically have the group begin praying for each other. Be sensitive to the Holy Spirit; this is His time. Keep the focus entirely on Him. Falling in love with God and hearing from Someone who loves them unconditionally is an incredible experience for young people. Let them listen and hear from Him!

Youth of this generation enjoy worship because it is real, and it is safe. God will never leave or forsake them.

On our church's annual youth retreat, we always have an optional time in the afternoon called "vespers." We usually have a few simple songs and then pray. One year, we had a couple of kids that were going to lead a few songs and then spend some time in prayer. Suddenly everything just got quiet. You could've heard a pin drop! People sat down quietly where they were and waited on the Lord. We stayed there, no one moving for about forty-five minutes. It became the highlight of the weekend for those who participated in it. It was an incredible time of meeting with God on a one-to-one basis. It became salt to make us thirsty for more!

No formula for worship

Like in anything else, there is no exact formula for worship. Instead, it is an attitude of the heart which becomes very personal.

As a youth worship leader, Hubie tried to give lots of room for experimenting with different styles of music, lighting effects, worshiping without music, and so on. Most of all, he tried to provide an environment of love and security for the young people. Youth cell is a great place to experiment with various worship experiences.

Our kids love to worship with the lights turned low. It helps them focus on God instead of each other and gives a feeling of intimacy.

If you have kids that can lead these times of worship and prayer, let them do it with some help from you, if needed. Kids enjoy being led by their peers. They don't demand excellence or the talent they would expect if an adult leads. They tend to overlook inexperience in their peers and enthusiastically support them in their endeavors.

Be led by the Spirit

A leader should not be afraid to give direction during the times of worship. He should never be controlling, but should be sensitive to the Holy Spirit. A leader should recognize when to offer some direction to the group. In the opening times of worship, direction adds security because people don't feel they have to guess about what to do.

Give time for kids to talk about what they are feeling during worship. Kids love to hear from their peers. You can take time to pray and then go back into worship. Prayer and worship go together as we see in Revelation 5:8, "Now when He had taken the scroll, the four living creatures and the twenty-four elders fell down before the Lamb, each having a *harp*, and golden *bowls* full of incense, which are the prayers of the saints." The *harps* of worship and the *bowls* of prayer go hand-in-hand. So in these times, the group may find themselves going back and forth between the two.

Worship is creative!

Youth cell groups and worship can go very well together, but not always. Sometimes if the group is too small, kids may feel too self-conscious to really express themselves in worship. Another draw-back may be the simple fact that there is no musician available to lead out with a guitar or keyboard. Not many kids get into singing acappella!

Good news! Youth cells don't have to include a "worship" time with a singer and an instrument. You can pick a psalm to read. Give them some quiet time to think about the verses, then pray and ask the youth to share which part speaks to them. Have everyone share something they are thankful for that day. There can be so much creativity with worship in cells.

- **Worship with a CD player can be a simple option.** You could play a set of songs where everybody stands and sings along. Make sure the volume is turned up high enough so everyone feels free to sing out! Ask the kids for song suggestions. Check your local Christian bookstore for CDs made for youth or ask for suggestions from the kids.

- **Pair up** with another cell group for a special night of worship. Or you can invite a guest worship leader to join you for the evening.

- **Take Turns!** Have everyone interested in helping with your cell's worship time be responsible for a cell night and lead the group.

- **Video Worship** Watch a music video or an actual worship service that has been video-taped (be careful not to let it get too long). Have everyone join in by listening or singing along. Using a video designed for children can bring lighthearted worship time filled with laughter and fond memories.

- **Sharing thoughts** After a really good time of worship, hand out index cards and encourage everyone to write down what he or she was thinking, but do not sign names. Read some of them to the group. This is another kind of creative sharing.

- **Communion** During worship, take communion together. Have someone strum the guitar or have an instrumental worship CD playing in the background. Each person meditates quietly on the Lord. Break bread by giving everyone a large chunk of bread from an unsliced loaf. Then encourage the youth to find ways to affirm each other—a hug or encouraging comment to share—as they break bread with others in the group.

Keep your eyes on Jesus

As youth spend time in the presence of God, the Holy Spirit helps them see themselves as they really are. He helps them to search their hearts and get their priorities back into perspective. It is a time of renewing the things that are valuable in their lives. Worship in cell, as well as youth celebration meetings, is a significant building block for the group as well as for the individuals.

Discover the value of helping youth get into the presence of God. As they spend time in His presence, you will see more growth than ever before in their lives. It does take time during the meeting or extra prayer on your part to see it happen, but the results are well worth it.

Bombard your City!

People in our city were stirred and amazed when more than 125 youth involved in cell groups at our church planned a week-long outreach/work project time for our city. On the first day, the youth pounded the sidewalks of the city and did spiritual warfare. They returned to share insights they gleaned concerning the strongholds of the city. The next day, they participated in work projects (with previous permission from the city) like removing a fence at a local baseball diamond, cutting down brush on the side of a creek and painting a refreshment stand in the park. Garbage was also picked up throughout the streets.

Homes were contacted in the city with questions like, "How could local churches serve you better? Have you ever had the Christian message explained to you in a way you understood"? On one of these door-to-door surveys, a cell member made contact with a single mom in desperate need of groceries. The woman in need was soon revisited with bags of groceries, and when the gospel was shared with her, she was ready to make a commitment to Christ.

Children's activities were planned in the park with refreshments and games. A basketball clinic for teens and a Christian band performed one evening. Many of these kids were quite open to discuss spiritual matters. Different types of people were reached throughout the week...from headbangers to skateboarders, grade school-age kids to the elderly, city officials to street people.

CHAPTER 9
Youth Missions and Outreach

J esus came to reconcile all mankind to the Father. He left us with a mission to make disciples called the Great Commission. The Great Commission must be part of our everyday lives. If we are not making disciples, what are we making? The Lord has commissioned us to make disciples among the nations and wants us to catch His heart for the world.

Today's youth have a lot of natural, built-in core values that could make it easy for them to go into missions. A radical call to forsake all and go into the harvest fields could satisfy the hunger they feel for realizing their purpose in life. A youth cell is the perfect place to build the character and vision that missionaries need.

As one young man told a group of youth leaders, "I am so tired of the least common denominator!" Rather than fulfilling only the minimum required in life, like many of today's youth, he was crying out for a strong sense of destiny and the challenge to fulfill it.

There are many resources available which enable us to teach missions to our youth cells in a practical and informative way. The following points are also useful when implementing missions as a life-style among youth.

Exposure

We need to continually expose our souls and spirits to Matthew 28:19, "Go therefore and make disciples of all nations, baptizing them in the name of the Son and of the Father and of the Holy Spirit, teaching them to observe all things that I have commanded you...." God shows us a big picture, bigger than our own backyards, even bigger than our own nation. We need to open our eyes to see, to become exposed!

Shocking images of spiritual and physical poverty are hard to forget. Hunger relief agencies have used this tool for years through television fund-raising campaigns. Teens need to realize that they really can make a difference in the world. Hanging out at the mall is not all there is to leading a fulfilled life.

Mark 16:15 tells us to, "Go into all the world and preach the good news to all creation." By exposing youth to the spiritual hunger in their own and other nations, they will be faced with the realities of unevangelized peoples.

A youth cell could take a day trip to a needy place in an area close to them. Visit a ministry: a drug treatment program, a pregnancy center, a homeless shelter, a ministry to truckers or teens. Tour and participate in activities or work projects they have.

Take a youth cell to a soup kitchen in an urban area or organization that ministers to people unlike themselves such as a children's home. Youth can share their "story" at those places.

Be bold to take them to the local highway and byways, the places that are crying out for the ministry of Jesus Christ. This will give them a chance to minister firsthand to other peoples. You may find you have gifted evangelists among your group!

Matthew 5:14-16 says, "You are the light of the world...." Allow them the opportunity to be lights in dark places they usually wouldn't go. This may involve a street outreach to the homeless in a large city! Usually areas considered to be "dangerous" have Christians already working there who know the approaches necessary to eliminate much of the danger. Respect their knowledge and help them accomplish what they are doing. God's people are everywhere.

Use the Internet, encyclopedias, dictionaries, statistics or maps. A big part of first experiences with missions is exposure, and sometimes that kind of exposure is what individuals need to make a life-changing decision. Have missionaries home on furlough speak at your cell or youth group: the personal touch does wonders! Let the youth ask questions about all the little-known details of missions joys and tears! Invite an exchange student to come to the cell and talk about his or her country. Cook up some snacks from other countries.

Jesus ministered—body, soul and spirit. We, too, need to minister to the whole person, supplying food, clothing, love, and the gospel. Talk about the things that are high priority, and low priority: get them thinking. Should we take clean water to the people, or teach them to make their water clean? Should we just pray for them or should we teach them to pray too? It's good to discuss moral issues versus cultural issues. You might find the youth have a more global perspective than you do!

Training

Once youth are educated about missions, you will find the need and desire for them to gain practical training in order for them to become effectively involved. If we don't train people, they will be standing in the field that's ready for harvest and they won't know how to pick the ripe fruit. Start with evangelism and how to share your faith in a practical way. (See "Sharing Your Testimony" on page 114.)

We have found it helpful to train the youth in confrontational evangelism, that is, sharing the gospel with people they don't know. If they can overcome the fear barrier of sharing the gospel with people they don't know, they will find it easier and more natural to evangelize their friends. (See "Evangelism Approach Questions," page 115.)

The focused prayer and preparation that goes into getting ready for this confrontational evangelism can cause accelerated growth and maturity in a short time. We have seen many life-changing experiences with God during evangelism "boot camps" consisting of three days of training and three days of evangelism.

Take time to have the youth share their testimonies with each other at cell group. Then challenge them to share it with someone outside the group. Learn scriptures that explain the plan of salvation.

Embracing missions

By now your group will have open eyes, open hands, and hopefully, open hearts. You will be able to challenge cell members to make a commitment before the Lord to be part of fulfilling the Great Commission. It's not everyone who may serve in a foreign country, but we are all called to fulfill the Great Commission. Once we have been exposed to the needs, what can we do? Don't leave the youth overwhelmed with the huge task. Have them take on their responsibility to pray for, financially support, or go to the people who do not know Jesus.

An important step toward missions is prayer. Pray regularly for those in your city who do not yet know Christ as well as for foreign mission. As a group, pick a region, missionary or unreached people group to support by praying consistently for them.

Find an organization with which they can partner in reaching the unreached peoples. Many will supply materials at your request. Send an offering from your cell group to one of them. Even a small one will build the cell's faith. They personally and corporately can make a difference. It can be a way in which people, who are still too young to go in full time missions, can effect other nations now. One cell did baby-sitting as a group and donated the money they raised to a missionary as a Christmas gift to her.

Another youth cell group supports a little girl through a child sponsorship program. It's a challenge for them to get the money together month after month, but they feel called to do it.

Maybe your group can "embrace" a missionary from your church, or a missionary in a country your group has vision for. Embracing is a close and personal touch between two individuals. Although the physical aspects of embracing cannot be done from afar, many other aspects of embracing can be. Show you care by sending letters as well as praying. Have the cell youth make birthday cards and artwork to send to your missionary. Commit to a year of interaction.

Take your cell on a mission trip

Why not take your cell on a trip to another nation? The planning, fund-raising, performing dramas, work projects and travel experiences will make an unforgettable experience. You can do it!

The following gives some practical tips about planning for and leading a short term missions team.

- **Where**—Decide, through prayer and discussion with your church leadership, where God wants your cell to go. Keep travel cost in mind as you pray.
- **Vision**—Write out a rough draft of your vision and purpose.
- **Get the OK**—Continue sharing your plans with your church leadership and missions department for their valuable input.
- **Do they want you?** Get a contact person from the place where you wish to take your group.
- **Dates and prices**—Set the dates and check into travel prices.
- **Strategy**—Find out the gifts and talents in your cell group and put them to work as you develop plans for the trip. Use musical gifts, leadership gifts, sports gifts, acting gifts, and anything else the Lord has placed in your group.
- **Team meetings**—Plan meetings for prayer and strategy outside of your regular cell meeting.
- **Money**—Do your fund-raising! Depending on costs of your trip, this may take quite a while. Get started early, perhaps a year ahead.
- **Training**—Do any necessary training with your team (language study, drama and mime practice).
- **GO!**
- **Report back to your church, family and friends!**

Natural missionaries

Be Spirit-led in your approach to teaching youth about world missions. Mission strategies are changing to a hands-on relational approach where local churches have a more intimate involvement in the mission. This natural connection allows for youth to "buy into" world missions to a greater degree than their parents. Today's group of mobile, globally minded, relational youth could be the greatest mission force of modern history!

Helpful Resources for Youth Missions
Betty Barnett, *Friend Raising*, (YWAM Publishing).
Patrick Johnstone, *Operation World*, (YWAM Publishing).
Peter Menzel, *Material World—A Global Family Portrait*, (Sierra Club Books).

What do they know?

One night at cell group, I read different stories and asked the cell group to discuss the scenarios. I was rather shocked by the kids responses. They did not give the answers I thought they would. I thought they knew more about God's standards for sexual purity than they really did.

The pastor heard about our discussion and responded by giving an entire Sunday morning message on sexual purity.

CHAPTER 10
Teaching Sexual
Purity in Youth Cells

O nce youth hit puberty, and often before, they begin thinking about the opposite sex. This attraction is normal and God-given. Without those feelings, few people would bother to get married or have children.

The questions that all of us have dealt with are the same that the youth of every generation deal with. What should I do with my feelings? How do I find the right person for me? Will anyone really ever like me? What will others think of me if I never find someone to marry? The world has many avenues for these questioning adolescents to take. There are numerous self-help books on the arts of finding your dream date, fantasy, masturbation and the like. Movies, music and television also contribute to the road of knowledge in the field of sexual relationships. Unfortunately most of these sources do not provide information from a biblical world view.

From adolescence on to marriage, this is probably one of the most consuming issues to youth. One young person knowingly remarked that when youth leaders want to increase attendance at youth group, they plan a meeting on the subject about sex!

Teaching is one thing, but practical accountability to help the teens walk in sexual purity is another. Surveys show that many Christian teens say sex before marriage is wrong, but are still actively involved in sexual relationships. There is something involved here beyond basic hypocrisy. A lot of it results from the relativistic world-view that bombards all of us daily in our Western culture.

Cultural relativism is expressed in the statements, "Whatever works for you..." and "If it works, it must be true." The proper response by Christians is to stand on their historical, biblical foundations, especially in the areas under attack—morality and truth.

In a world muddled and muddied by relativism, historical, biblical foundations will at first be criticized as narrow and intolerant, but then be welcomed as a breath of fresh air. As everything else becomes blurred, a young believer's uncompromising stand for sexual purity will provide hope and good news for a world searching for an anchor to latch onto.

In the traditional youth group, a lot of youth leaders won't even know who or how long their teens have been dating. But in youth cells, these are natural topics of discussion and prayer as youth are discipled. Relationships provide the trust for tough questions to be asked of youth who are dating.

Youth cell groups provide the venue for practical accountability while the youth are involved with the opposite sex in dating relationships.

Speak loudly and clearly

Youth leaders need to be a voice in this maze of sexual issues. They need to speak loudly and clearly declaring a standard of righteousness for the youth of this generation. They need to admonish youth to stand up and make the right decisions, to walk away from the places that promote sexual promiscuity, and to flee youthful lusts.

Questions will always arise that youth leaders can't answer simply by reading one scripture verse. What do leaders do with these gray areas? It's far easier to just make rules, but some areas are right for one person, and wrong for the other. Parents may have standards already set for their family for some of these issues. Youth leaders need to teach youth to hear from God, their parents and to listen to input from other godly people. When young people seek God's standards, the fruit is much more lasting and these godly principles will be reproduced over and over again in all areas of their lives.

Fear of the Lord

Teens today know the consequences of a life-style or even just one fling with sexual sin. They can see the negative effects of teen pregnancy and are aware of the dangers of sexually transmitted disease. These unwanted side effects show us some of the reasons why God wants us to be sexually pure. But more than the fear of pregnancy or STD's, we desire to see youth with the fear of the Lord in their hearts—youth who live pure lives because of their love for God, not because they fear getting AIDS.

Having a reverence for the Lord in our lives empowers us to overcome sin's temptation. Discipline may last for a season, but one experience can begin the downward spiral for even the most disciplined person. For some, sex can become addictive. And outside of marriage, it's like any other sin—devastating! It brings pain and destruction in people's lives and in the heart of our Lord. We need to ask God for such a great love for Him and His Word that we will obey no matter what the cost may be (see John 14:15,21).

> Having a reverence for the Lord in our lives empowers us to overcome sin's temptation.

While giving Christian youth boundaries of purity, chastity and abstinence, we need to address the following areas.

Sexual attraction

An area often not addressed is sexual attraction. The reality is that we as humans are created to be attracted to those of the opposite sex. It is normal and not evil to feel this attraction. What a person chooses to do with these feelings makes it negative or positive. Our emotions and responses are God-given. It's the way our bodies work. It's all part of the process of our sexuality. Sexual intimacy is a gift from God to demonstrate communion, connectedness and oneness. We need to teach the youth to control the process when they don't have the parameters in which to complete it—a marriage relationship involving one man and one woman for a lifetime.

Self-control is a lifelong practice, not something that ends with marriage. We often use the phrase "sexual purity until marriage" when discussing sexual matters with young people. The truth is we need sexual purity after marriage as well. Youth may be shocked to learn that even married adults need to control their thought lives. Giving practical ways to escape falling into the trap of lust, without losing their humanness, is vital.

Youth need to feel free to talk of their attractions (privately) with youth cell leaders. This will help them process and recognize these feelings for what they are.

Same sex attraction

Statistics vary widely, claiming anywhere from one to ten percent of teens are gay or lesbian, experiencing some degree of homosexual feelings or curiosities. In your youth cells and groups there will be those youth who are struggling with their sexual identity, that is, feeling attracted to the same sex. These teens need to know they can turn to their leaders for help. While the Bible plainly teaches homosexual behavior is sinful (Romans 1:26-27), the label "homosexual" should not be based on a teen's feelings, attractions, or impulses. Often these feelings are latent and have not been acted upon.

Understanding and wise guidance can make the difference in helping those attracted to the same sex to avoid homosexual activity altogether. The same compassion and gentleness is needed to help in restoring those who may already be caught in sin (Galatians 6:1).

Offer as much help as you can to see the teen set free. Help may include a Christian counselor. You will want to work with your pastor to find a recommended professional.

Christian teens struggling with their sexuality feel alienated and often unwelcomed in youth groups, especially if they hear cruel jokes. Youth leaders must follow the example of Jesus and His response to the adulteress woman, and like one leader said, "Turn our youth groups from places of stone-throwing into refuges of hope."

"Teens can be encouraged that showing God's love to gay and lesbian friends does not mean they are spiritually compromising: it means they are witnessing. By modeling God's heart for homosexuals, your youth group can become a beacon of light that breaks through religious stereotypes and demonstrates the same radical love Jesus showed."[1]

The Bible provides hope for every sinner. Everyone is equally in need of God's grace. No matter what the sin, always point the teen toward Jesus and help him or her in the healing process.

How to stay pure

A little song children learned in Sunday School clearly illustrates some of the practical ways we can teach youth to avoid sexual impurity. It goes like this, "Be careful little eyes what you see, there's a Father up above, watching over us in love, so be careful little eyes what you see." It goes on to include the ears, hands, feet and mouth with its timeless advice. Youth cell leaders need to encourage cell members to be careful in these very areas with some of the following advice:

Eyes: Be careful what you allow your eyes to see. Magazines, scenes on TV, or on the Web: whether it's a frequent bad habit or a onetime event, your experiences through your eye-gate can lead you into fields you need to avoid.

Ears: Be careful what music, conversations at school and the workplace you listen to.

Hands: Be careful what you touch. Some touch can be blatantly seductive; some may seem innocent, but behind it may be a heart looking for more. As leaders, we need discernment in this area, and so do our youth.

Mouth: Be careful of the conversations and the kind of jokes you participate in.

Feet: Be careful where you go. The kind of parties and movies you go to influence and mold you.

Mixed gender cells should separate so guys and girls can talk candidly about how they are doing in these areas. This should be followed by prayer.

It's impossible to make hard and fast rules for places youth should and should not go, but we can give principles that will enable them to think and pray through opportunities they are given. Joseph gives us a valuable lesson in self-control as a good-looking single man who encountered sexual temptation. When Potiphar's wife grabbed him, he ran and left his coat behind. He didn't take time to pray about it. He already knew what his standard was before he got in the situation. "Flee also youthful lusts; but pursue righteousness, faith, love, peace with those who call on the Lord out of a pure heart" (II Timothy 2:22).

Encourage teens to determine their standards for purity before they get into a tempting situation. It is too easy to rationalize when you are in the heat of the situation. You must decide beforehand what your actions will be. It's like setting your alarm clock for a certain time, but not determining if you will get up when it goes off. You won't get up! Your mind will rationalize and come up with a hundred reasons for sleeping in.

Encourage the youth to hear from God, parents and other godly people as they set their standards. Write them down! The cell group is the perfect place for this. Then youth leaders can hold them accountable to what God has told them to do. This is true biblical accountability. It is not telling people what to do, but keeping them accountable for what God has told *them* to do.

> Encourage the youth to hear from God, parents and other godly people as they set their standards.

Sex education in church

Consider getting all your youth cells together annually and going through a relationship series. Because this is a sensitive issue, it's important to notify parents ahead of time that you are planning to discuss this topic. At our relationship series, we talk about attraction, lust, masturbation, accountability, purity, dating, and praying for a marriage partner. Several adults, young and old, from the church share their testimonies in the area of relationships. This is a fun time, as well as a real eye-opener for the youth. They realize they are not so different after all. We plan a time when the girls and guys are separated to talk about issues each sex deals with on a more specific level. This also enables the teachers to talk more personally.

We go through a questionnaire that challenges the youth to think about what type of person they want to marry, and in turn what kind of people they want to date if they do want to date. (See "Could This Be the One?" page 119). We have questions and answers, some written anonymously, some asked verbally, within the big group to see where the kids are concerning sex (See "Sex and You," page 118 for a questionnaire sample). We also have prayer and ministry time which often ends up growing from week to week as the series progresses.

It is a challenge as a leader to talk about the area of purity. A leader has to be willing to be vulnerable so the youth will be able to share their experiences. It is exciting to see youth walking in purity, free from the bondage of past relationships and the pressure to date. It is gratifying to see young guys free from the bondage of lust and pornography. What a blessing it is to see two young people walk into marriage as pure individuals. It is a possible dream, and we can declare it so.

Freedom from past relationships

One area that we can easily overlook is freedom from past relationships. It's sad to see so many teens having babies. For as many as deliver a baby, there are many more who are sexually active. Unfortunately, many churches carry the presumption that "our youth" are not like that. Let's not be naive. The world today is obsessed with sex, and our youth are affected by its influence. Even the grip of pornography has been strengthened by the Internet's easy access. Let's face reality head on and offer what Jesus offers— repentance, forgiveness and freedom!

After a purity teaching, don't leave a group of youth sitting there and wishing it wasn't too late for them. There are, and there will always be, those who hear the message after they have lost their virginity. Let's preach the Word without compromise. Let's preach purity, but let's also offer freedom to those who are willing to repent. Romans 2:4 says that it is His kindness that leads us to repentance. It should be our kindness that offers that repentance.

Do not think that the damaging effects of sexual sin will simply go away. Help the teen accept Christ's forgiveness and set new healthy boundaries for him or her. As tough as true change in habits can be, not choosing to change can result in lifelong struggles that are much harder in the long run. Here again, weekly or bi-weekly youth cell meetings give leaders the contact that is needed to help youth walk through the repentance and healing process.

Godly role models

We highly recommend that youth cell leaders constantly look for ways to relevantly share about sexual purity. Godliness and purity are contagious. As youth cell leaders model sexual purity by developing a vibrant, satisfying relationship with the Lord, the young people around them cannot help but be influenced. Being in relationship with Christ, and knowing Him intimately produces sexual purity. As we enjoy the benefits of walking with Christ in freedom from sexual addictions and bondages, others will want the same contentment.

Married youth leaders can set a godly standard and help kids have an idea what God intended when He created marriage by caring for their spouse and guarding their own marriage from decay. Teens may not have seen a Christ-centered marriage up close before.

Regularly addressing sexual issues biblically will strengthen the youth in the daily fight for purity in an impure world.

Helpful Sexual Purity Resources:

Steve and Mary Prokopchak, *Called Together:* A Marriage Preparation Workbook, (House to House Publications: Ephrata, PA, 1994). Tele: 800-848-5892.
John White, *Eros Redeemed, Breaking the Stranglehold of Sexual Sin,* (InterVarsity Press: Downers Grove, Illinois, 1993).
Josh McDowell & Bob Hostetler, *Handbook for Counseling Youth,* (Word Publishing, 1996). Includes chapters on Sexual Issues and Abuse.

Notes

[1] Kelli Trujillo, "Called to the Closet, God's Heart for Gay and Lesbian Youths," *Youthworker,* November/December 1999, p. 46.

Wanted: Real Relationships

I glanced around the circle of youth sitting in our living room. Their only response to my third kickoff question for cell group was a blank stare. What happened to our alive, growing, energetic youth cell group?

It had been so full of life. In fact, this was the first meeting after the multiplication. We had just commissioned out a new youth cell. Everyone had seemed excited about it.

Then it dawned on me. I didn't know these kids very well. I had no relationship with them. As youth cell leaders, my wife and I had spent most of our time with our two assistant leaders who were now leading the new youth cell we had commissioned out. Not only that, but most of the more mature youth had gone along with them to start the new cell. They were the ones who had done most of the talking, teaching and planning for the group.

I realized that our multiplication resulted **in two *new* youth cells.** Each of the cells needed a fresh start, building relationships and functioning as its own group. For us, it was back to the drawing board, literally! At the next youth cell meeting, we played Pictionary, a game where participants draw pictures and others guess what they are drawing.

We needed to build relationship with these kids. We needed to get to know them. What are their gifts? What are their talents? Do they have a relationship with God? What is God's call on their lives? How can we help them fulfill that call? And so, the life cycle of a new youth cell begins.

CHAPTER 11
Help! "Idea Grab Bag" for Youth Cell Groups

G od, the Creator, is a creative God who wants to shower His people with creativity. Youth cell groups need to be fresh and alive with God's creative potential.

This "grab bag" of ideas will help youth cell members become more actively involved in each other's lives—to be in relationship—as they reach out with the love of Jesus.

Share your testimony

Hearing what God has done in others' lives is encouraging and gives hope to others. It also helps cell members get to know one another. When a new cell starts, have one or two people share their personal testimony at each cell meeting.

Encourage a youth that no matter how simple and unimpressive his or her testimony seems, there is power in it! It's great to be able to say, "I became a Christian at four years of age and have been serving God ever since."

Another option is to have each person share a story of when they saw God at work in his or her life.

Complete the sentence

Start the cell meeting with an open-ended sentence to get the young people to share personal items from their lives. Here are some

Help! Idea Grab Bag for Youth Cell Groups

85

examples to pick from, some to chuckle over and some to provoke thought:

Lighthearted or humorous beginnings
"An embarrassing moment for me was when..."
"One of the best times of my life was..."
"My favorite teacher is..."
"If I had a million dollars I would..."
"My idea of a perfect date is..."
"What I want for Christmas is..."
"When I am 70 years old, I want to be doing..."
"One thing I enjoy about this cell group is... "

Sharing
"I want to thank God for..."
"What I'm thankful for this week is..."
"Someone blessed me by doing..."
"My toughest experience happened when..."
"I'm working at...in my life."
"Some personal vision I have for my life is..."
"At school, I'm praying for..."
"In the future, I would like to serve God by..."
"What God is speaking personally to me is..."
"I am reaching out to..."
Listen to specific needs, then pray for them as a group.

Clash party
Have a "clash night" to see who can dress the worst. Give a silly prize such as gummie worms to the top winner. Then discuss peer pressure and judging others by their appearance.

Spreading cheer
Go as a cell group to the local home for the elderly. Plan a drama, dress up as clowns or take board games. Ask your contact there about bringing small gifts to the residents and ask for suggestions. They could be homemade ones made on another cell evening—a cookie, a decorative magnet or card with a Bible verse

on it. Spend time talking to the elderly and listening to their joys and sorrows. Their smiles will be reward enough for your time and efforts there! *You* may be the one with the biggest smile!

Skate night

Several youth cells could combine to rent the local roller skating rink for the night. A week earlier, post or hand out flyers announcing a free skate to all the kids in the town. Halfway through the skate, perform a mime that introduces the kids to Jesus, and spend the night building relationships with the kids.

Lend a hand

A work project is always a blessing to those who participate. One youth cell had a great time when they spent a day painting a house for a legally blind man who had to spend 10 months in the Veterans Hospital. Be careful to pick a project within your cell group's reach. Frustration can result if the project is too difficult or takes too long to complete. Ask other adults or parents to help out.

Youth in charge

Have some youth cells lead the Sunday morning services at your church. They can lead worship, perform a dance complete with fancy footwork—whatever! It will give the "old folks" a better perspective on today's youth culture! It is sure to be an encouragement to all as the youth testify of God's answers to prayer in their lives. Give the rest of the congregation the opportunity to agree with them in prayer for others' needs. Take a night to pray and plan.

Beach party

Hold a winter beach party at your cell meeting. Hand out leis and dress in shorts (turn the heat up!). Spread out a checked table cloth on the floor and start with a picnic dinner or snack, followed with games. Participate in a time of worship and dance.

Plan a tournament!

Play basketball, pool, ping-pong, cards or whatever you have access to. Start the tournament after the teaching time and possibly

Help! Idea Grab Bag for Youth Cell Groups

87

span several cell meeting nights. Attach a nice prize to the first-place winner's slot. Make sure to allow sufficient time after the teaching...get started on time!

Show 'em you really care!

Youth are involved in all kinds of extra curricular activities. Support fellow cell members by attending sporting events or musical concerts. By seeing that person in a different setting other than youth cell, you can gain a greater understanding of that person's gifts. Even if only two or three are able to go, it's still worth the effort to support and honor that cell member with your time. As a youth cell leader, try to attend an extracurricular activity your cell members participate in.

Progressive suppers

Divide up a meal between several homes. You could pick a western, picnic or holiday theme. An international theme could have each home serving a dish from a different country. Meet as a group to travel to each home, progressing through your meal. Parents or others from your congregation could serve as hosts.

Hikers and bikers

Bodies need to be exercised as well as your spirit. Tell the youth to bring a little money for a snack, and walk to a local ice cream shop or corner store. Relax and enjoy your treat together.

Another option is to pick a spring or fall day and go for a bike hike or walking hike with your cell members. Take along packed lunches and don't forget to invite those you are reaching out to! Take pleasure in God's creation as you strengthen your relationships with each other. Halfway through the scenic hike, stop at a picturesque spot and have an outdoor worship service.

Car wash

Get together and wash each other's cars for a fun and practical way to build relationships. Invite everyone to bring along hoses, soap, buckets, and the like. Buy air fresheners to give to everybody to put in their fresh, clean car.

I love ya, man!

Simply spend time together while sitting on the lawn or the porch after a cell meeting. Have a picnic, swim party, go shopping or roller skating. Nothing deeply spiritual, but relationship-building! Ask your group for inexpensive suggestions.

Sound hunt

Divide into groups and supply each group with a battery-operated tape recorder and a list of sounds to capture on tape: a cow mooing, parents kissing, a siren, an airplane taking off, a fly buzzing—the sky is the limit! The first group back with the most sounds from the list, wins!

Gag me with a spoon!

Have the youth plan a mystery dinner and invite their parents. The mystery menu would include secret names for the food and utensils, so the parents might inadvertently order green beans with chocolate cake for their first course. Have the youth serve their parents all three courses.

Harvest party

Plan a fall party in a barn or garage on a cool night, complete with straw bales and pumpkins. Enjoy silly group games. Break out the hot cider and other harvest munchies. A great addition is a bonfire to warm up to, along with hot dogs and marshmallows to roast. Our group has this traditional party the evening before Thanksgiving. The college kids who come home for the holiday break join us. Conversations last late into the night.

An educational competition

Divide the youth into groups or compete as individuals. Have Bible memorization contests where the winners earn prizes such as a CD or tickets to a concert.

Overnight camping trip

This doesn't have to be a lot of work. You could even have a very memorable camp-out in someone's backyard! Call on resources of experienced campers in the congregation.

A guy and girl thing

Take the girls on a shopping trip (near or far) and let the guys play basketball and snack on pizza at someone's house.

Decorate a Christmas tree

Have the group make homemade decorations, popcorn strings, creative ornaments and decorate a tree for a Christian ministry. Present it to them a few weeks before Christmas so they can enjoy it the whole season!

Women of virtue

Teach a course on etiquette for the girls, covering topics such as hair care, manicures, fine dining skills and shopping tips. Talk about godly femininity. Use others from your congregation as resource people. Plan a special banquet for the girls and their mothers at the close of the course.

Ideas for fellowship

- Food activities: dinner with parents, barbecues in the park, ice cream sundae parties, make your own pizza parties
- Work activities: serving a needy person in the church, trash pickup, community service, etc.
- Sports activities: skiing, wacky Olympics, volleyball
- Plan a party or outreach and invite another youth cell or adult cell group

Liven Up Cell Teachings!

What's your answer?

Find several intriguing or controversial questions from an advice column in the newspaper or teen magazine. Read each question and have the youth write up their response based on the Bible, using at least one scripture. Compare their responses with the columnist's answers. Discuss conflicting views.

Another option: have the kids each write questions they may have. Divide up in groups and answer them. Must include scripture!

Object lessons

Use objects to help illustrate your lesson. When talking about gossip, use a cow tongue (from the local butcher) as a visual illustration—sure never to be forgotten!

A lesson about the importance of the things we say could be illustrated by trying to get some toothpaste back in the tube—"it's impossible to take something back once we've said it."

Bring a newspaper in a small bag. Have someone crumple up each sheet and then try to put it back in the bag. "Mistakes do matter." Encourage the kids to live their lives carefully.

Current events

Choose a current event as a subject and apply biblical principles. Talk about the AIDS crisis. Discuss problems in the nation or in the world, such as a recent earthquake or political uprising. Ask the kids for advice they would give the leader of their country. Have the kids find verses that relate to these events.

Lighten up!

Incorporate humor, one-liners, proverbs, and quotes in your teachings to keep the interest of teens. Bring a cartoon!

Help! Idea Grab Bag for Youth Cell Groups

91

Very special guests

Invite speakers to come and minister to your cell group:

- Your pastor
- A missionary
- A prophetically-gifted person
- An evangelist
- Someone with the gift of teaching
- Have someone from a local ministry share
- Have someone from the church or even the cell itself share something intriguing they do.

Ask guests for permission to ask questions about their work in ministry. Allow time for discussion. These questions are only the beginning:

- What is your pet peeve?
- What is the greatest thing that has ever happened to you?
- What is the most disappointing?

Ideas for prayer times

- Teach youth to pray, what to pray for, and for whom to pray. Pray often. Model a life-style of prayer right in the cell group.
- Invite prayer requests at the beginning, in the middle of or at the close of cell group. Ask for testimonies to answered prayers.
- Keep a cell group prayer journal.
- Pray through scriptures. (Personalize Colossians 1:3-14.)
- Do a prayer walk or drive through your community. Stop at strategic places. Pray as God leads you, and then move on. Take time to debrief at the close of your time together.
- Have a prayer meeting. Plan a creative course of action: prayer stations, prayer partners, worship in between, etc.

Basic Values

The salvation message

This is the first foundation stone in a person's walk with God. Talk to each person individually to make sure they are confident of their own salvation.

Use teaching time in your group for this important issue. Make sure cell members know how to share their faith. (You may be shocked with what you find out.)

Memorize verses together to help equip every believer. Give role plays and examples of what to say (See "Sharing Your Testimony" on page 114).

Challenge the youth to personally fulfill the Great Commission themselves by sharing personal stories and giving insights from their own lives.

Every year we plan a boot camp for the DOVE youth. We bring the youth together to first spend time strengthening their personal walk with God. Then after a day or so, we move on to sharpening evangelism skills. The last part of the week, and the high point, is outreach, where we work with inner city ministries. We see our faith put into action...an absolutely unbeatable combination.

Baptism

Encourage every believer in your cell group to be baptized. Don't assume everyone understands what baptism is about even if they have grown up in the church.

Spend an evening sharing scriptures about the importance of baptism and set a date for the event to happen if there are cell members ready to take this important step.

Make sure parents are informed about this important step. Family and friends can be invited to celebrate this important landmark event.

After the baptism, have a festive snack. If it's held at a pool, invite everybody to go swimming and have a picnic later.

Important issues

Youth of every part of the world and history face certain challenges simply because they are young, making them unique from the rest of the population. Some issues will be similar from one generation to the next while others will be unique. Here is a list of several issues important to youth which need to be discussed from time to time.

Relationship with God	Sex
Prayer /hearing God's voice	Overcoming temptation
Baptisms	Practical Christian life-style
Faith	Evangelism
Missions	Worship
Finances	Spiritual gifts
Relationship with parents	Ministry development
Relationship with peers	Vision of your church
Personal vision statement	Accountability and authority
Healing and deliverance	

Outreach ideas
Ideas for outreach and evangelism

- Street witnessing or community door-to-door surveys
- Drama or puppetry in public areas
- Outreach to nursing homes, hospitals, etc.
- Local mission trips
- Watch the church bulletin for outreaches to join in on with the entire congregation. Go as a cell group.
- Together sponsor a child or missionary on a monthly basis
- Letter writing to prisoners, missionaries or college students

Project money box

Decide on a ministry or project your cell group would like to support. Commission one of the artistic or creative youth to make a collection box. For example: if your cell is raising money for a homeless shelter, cut out faces of people who live a life of poverty. Display the box at each cell meeting. Encourage cell members to place money in it when they can. Work toward a goal together.

Celebrate when you have reached the goal. Pray over your gift before sending it on.

Join the parade!

A few cells join together to construct a float to participate in your community's local parade. Come up with a creative theme together. Decorate the float with Jesus banners and balloons. Proclaim the good news in a straightforward, easy-to-understand way.

Picnic evangelism

Cell members invite unsaved friends and relatives for a picnic in a local park. Provide the food and fellowship! Bring a volleyball net.

Love in bloom!

Plant a few flowers in inexpensive clay pots or homemade planters to share with others. Pray over the pots together as a cell group. Send one pot home with each person to give to someone they are reaching out to. Bless someone!

Breakfast, anyone?

To raise money for a short-term mission trip or for a mission project, plan a continental breakfast for all those attending a Sunday morning service. The cell group(s) provides muffins, orange juice and coffee and displays a decorated basket for people to drop in donations. Provide information, by way of large posters, telling what project the money will go for.

A tournament for missions

Sponsor a volleyball or basketball tournament, along with one or two other cell groups. Invite other youth groups. Charge a small entrance fee and use the monies raised to be a prize purse. The winning team decides what ministry or missionary receives the cash.

Our Junior High Ministry Team

Our cell group of mostly junior highers meets in my basement. The youth love to wrestle each other into my old couch and toss the bean bag chair at each other. I smile at the explosions of energy. This is energy God wants to use for His glory. My basement is not a holding tank for a future ministry team. We are ministers of the gospel now! Our group sure does look different than the other adult cells. But we do many of the same things; pray for each other, take turns sharing and teaching. We don't have to wait 'til tomorrow...we're doing it today!

CHAPTER 12
Junior High Cell Groups

The junior high crowd is often a unique challenge for a youth leader. The youngest kids have just moved up from the children's ministry—you may think that some of them should still be there! Like most groups within the church, the junior high ministry team has the privilege of ministering to spiritually mature and spiritually immature Christians at the same time. But with junior highers, you can also have drastic differences in physical and emotional maturity as well. The challenge for you as the group leader is to reach the whole spectrum. Wow! You only have two or three years with the kids, but lots of changes can happen with the kids individually as well as how the group interacts with each other.

How can this highly energized group fit into the cell group structure? Transition from childhood to the teenage years can be a rocky road for the kids as well as for the youth leaders. Short attention spans, erratic emotions, awkwardness, growth spurts and overreaction can create chaos. Not everyone is able to appreciate silly comments this age group can regularly erupt with.

But tremendous potential lies with this vulnerable age group ready to explode into the world. These young teens, going through this transitional time, often are very flexible, making them more pliable in God's hands. Sure, sometime adults can get nervous when teens experiment and make life up as they go, but face it, this group, with their young zeal, can wreak havoc on the kingdom of darkness! Don't worry about perfection. Be sensitive to your group and its changing needs. Encourage and challenge the kids to spiritual maturity but don't expect it to happen overnight. Pray for your group and watch what God does. Some kids may surprise you with insightful questions and spiritual depth. Don't treat them like babies. Even though they still look childlike, don't underestimate them! They may be spiritually hungry and ready to run at an intense spiritual pace.

Role models

What junior highers often need are older, more mature youth and adults to channel their enthusiasm in the right direction and support them. Don't miss the opportunity of seeing the years of these young people filled with godly training. These youth are capable ministers in their own way. Don't make them wait until they grow up to be a part of home cell group ministry.

Parents need to be involved in the decision-making processes concerning which cell group the youth attend. They may require their child to remain in the intergenerational cell with them even though his or her friends are in a youth cell.

With parental consent, younger teens can join in with the youth cells already in existence. The older youth naturally mentor the younger who are looking for role models. Of course, the leader of that cell and the cell members must be in favor of having this age group join the cell because younger teens are less emotionally mature.

Some older youth who are newly saved or dealing with personal problems may not be ready to give to younger youth. Also, if older brothers and sisters are in a cell group, they may not want their younger siblings part of the group. In this case, starting a new cell made up exclusively of young teens may be advantageous.

All their own

The option of creating a new cell just for the young teens can be an excellent way to grow, adding new cells. In a cell of their peers, young teens can be themselves. Kids are shaped by their peer environment. Young teen cells can create an influential peer-to-peer environment where kids can mature spiritually. An older youth could lead the cell or assist the cell. One of the younger kids themselves could serve as an assistant.

Use available resources

Christian bookstores offer some very good materials designed especially for junior high. Read up on how to relate to this age group. Use these things creatively for your meetings. Regular Sunday School curriculum can be used for cell group. Change them to more specifically meet the needs of your group and have a relational emphasis.

Books: Books include ideas for all kinds of creative games, skits, retreats or meetings. We often use the books for a starting place and add our own ideas. Books for adults who wish to better understand young teens are also available.

Magazines: Some are for youth leaders, some for parents or some for teens only—it's all available! And the quality is good.

Videos to rent or buy: Teachings by Josh McDowell, Focus on the Family, etc. are great. A short Compassion International or mission video designed for adults can work with the youth, too! Take time to pray after viewing. Use the movies out there with caution, though. Some of them may not appeal to the kids. It's essential to preview all tapes before showing. Even a recommended film could contain some unpleasant surprises.

Teaching tips

Content: You really can feed good doses of the Word to the kids, but not for one hour straight. Teach and then reinforce with creative things such as object lessons, related games and quizzes (boys against the girls!). Our junior highers loved hearing the Old Testament stories not appropriate for younger children.

Don't lead a cell group or class alone: Have another responsible person along to help deal with discipline while you keep the rest of the group moving. Not allowing a problem person to control the group takes away some of the fun of misbehaving or acting out.

Object lessons: They are great! Use simple ones or more complicated ones. Use some you remember from your own children's church days! Bring in a small animal trap or even a mouse trap and talk about the enemy's traps for our lives.

Have guests: Someone new freshens things up! Junior highers seem to respect a new face. Have an adult who hunts dress up in full garb and show his bow and arrow and then talk about the arrows of the enemy (Ephesians 6:16). Have someone on the senior high wrestling team talk about how they live out their faith with the team. Invite the pastor out for questions and answers. Silly questions like, "What's your favorite flavor of ice cream?" help kids personally relate to him.

Keep 'em interested

Youth leader Sarah started a junior high class during her church's Sunday morning celebration because she felt like the kids were tuning out much of the teaching that happened there—especially the youngest who had just left children's ministry. "Cell groups provide some teaching, but at the Sunday morning class, the primary purpose is teaching. We meet two Sundays a month, after the worship time with the congregation. We encourage the kids on the other Sundays not to lose focus or miss the opportunity to learn by listening to the regular message."

Sarah also started a junior high youth group where they all come together. She felt it was important for the kids to develop broader peer relationships as well as the close-knit ones in the cell group. The group does a service project or recreational activity once a month.

The Christian youth involved in our cell groups like nothing better than coming into a cell group meeting, having a welcoming statement, and then being told the meeting is moving to another location. Perhaps we decide to conduct a street prayer walk or help some small group member with a project. The kids love that kind of spontaneity!

Set goals!

Think through your objectives for each activity whether fun or serious. Keep the goals simple and keep all the activities wrapped around them. Don't forget the original purpose, but don't be afraid to shift them when the need arises. Sarah adds, "The highlight of the year always ends up being our annual retreat!"

CHAPTER 13
From Teen Cell Leaders, For Teen Cell Leaders

Written by two teen youth cell leaders: Sarah Gehman of DOVE Christian Fellowship Ephrata-Lititz, Pennsylvania, and Julie Mitchell of Indianapolis Christian Fellowship, Indiana.

Sometimes it is very difficult being an assistant leader to kids my own age," says Sarah. "I don't always know the answers to problems or questions that cell members have, but my advice is to *admit it*! I don't act like I have the answers if I really don't. I know that, as a leader, I will quickly lose the respect of my cell members if I act like a 'know it all,' and it won't solve any problems. I tell them I don't know, but I will ask my advisors about the situation, if they don't mind. Sometimes they don't even want an answer necessarily, they just want someone to listen to them. Listening is very important! Just do your best; no one will ask for more than that from you!"

"During my time as a teen cell leader," says Julie, "I often struggled with how to be a friend and a leader at the same time. When conflicts came up or decisions needed to be made, sometimes it was hard for me to exercise the authority I had as a leader, and sometimes it was hard for my close friends to respect me as their leader."

Although leading a cell group can be daunting for a teenager, and presents its own unique problems, mature teenagers make excellent leaders of their peers when given the opportunity. They have the privilege of being trained from the ground up to minister to others at a young age, which serves to greatly strengthen them spiritually and emotionally. In this chapter, Sarah and Julie share some of the valuable lessons the Lord taught them while they dealt with the issues of leading a cell group of their peers.

Humble leadership

Teen cell leaders need to realize that they lead because God has called them, not because of their own merit. Peers respond positively to humble, gentle leadership, not to controlling dictatorship. A leader must remember that the Lord delights in working through a meek spirit (James 4:6).

Flexibility

One of the most important aspects of being a youth cell leader is being flexible. "Teens are not always predictable, so we must be prepared to deal with the unexpected, spontaneous situations and/or problems calmly without getting stressed out," says Sarah. "Nothing is more frustrating than having a leader get upset because things didn't go the way she wanted them to." Teen leaders have to learn to do their best and keep a good attitude, no matter what.

Getting respect

Teen leaders must respect those in authority over them; they can't expect peers to respect them as leaders if they refuse to honor their own authorities. This includes not only youth group and church leaders but also parents and the parents of cell members. Even if parents are not Christians, God commands us to submit to them, and He will honor our obedience (Ephesians 6:1-3).

If a teen cell leader is blessed with godly parents, he should communicate with them about the cell. "I found that when I wasn't willing to talk to my parents about my cell, the cell itself suffered," said Julie. "When I was willing to communicate with them, my parents were a wonderful source of insight, encouragement and support."

If a teen leader cannot talk to his parents, he should talk to another adult to keep him accountable and support him with prayer. A leader's example of respect for authority will speak more effectively than any words.

Dealing with feelings of inadequacy

"Throughout my years as a teen leader, my biggest struggle was with feelings of inadequacy," said Julie. "I hesitated to become a leader because I wasn't sure that I could hear God's voice. When I was a leader, I was often discouraged because I felt like no matter what I did, I could never accomplish everything to please everyone. It seemed like other cell leaders had exciting things to share about what God was doing in their cells, while my cell was the same old, same old. Even if I did everything right, planned every detail, called every person, and prayed for hours, something was lacking."

Julie's outlook started to change when she realized that being a cell leader was not about succeeding, but about pouring out her life in obedience to the Lord. She learned to be confident in Christ. Rather than looking at herself and her weaknesses and failures, she pressed toward God who desired to work through her. He was the One who had called her. Now Julie began to have the faith that He would speak to her (Jeremiah 29:13).

> Julie started to focus on finding vision for her cell. Then she worked toward carrying out that purpose without comparing herself to others.

Julie started to focus on finding vision for her cell. Then she worked toward carrying out that purpose without comparing herself to others. In addition, she started focusing on loving her members rather than pleasing them and trying to meet their expectations. She realized that while a leader must be teachable and open to criticism and correction, she could never make everyone happy all the time. Her security needed to come solely from Christ as she obeyed the Lord. Doing this, she had no reason to feel inadequate or ashamed (II Timothy 2:15).

Involvement

Making sure that each member of the cell feels as though they are a vital part of the group is important in keeping a healthy cell. If even one person feels unneeded, they most likely will eventually stop coming or stop actively participating in discussions, activities or social times. This will be a loss for the cell as a whole.

"Feeling a part of the group is essential for all of us," says Sarah. "Recognize that not everyone is gifted in the same areas. Youth tend to get down on themselves because they are not as athletic or as musical as someone else. I have done a teaching on fruits of the Spirit and gifts of the Spirit to help my cell see their potential.

"Then I focus on each person's unique talents and gifts. I ask some kids to teach, help with worship, host a cell at their house, or bring a snack. Even though it is like pulling teeth at first to get some kids to participate, they will get more excited about helping the more they experience it." Positive involvement helps to keep the youth interested and active while helping to take some of the load off the leader's shoulders.

Activities

Sarah discovered that being active as a cell was beneficial. Her cell started helping with an evening children's outreach. "It has really strengthened our cell and caused us to grow as a group and individually," says Sarah. "The focus has been taken off of us and placed on the kids with whom we are working."

Serving others is always a good idea! Whether a cell helps in a soup kitchen, retirement home, or goes on prayer walks, serving together within their community is important.

When deciding service activities, take into account a cell's gifts and interests. No matter what is decided, don't be surprised if some kids are less than enthusiastic. Don't worry, give it a try and see if they don't start liking it after a time or two!

While participating in service activities, have goals and spend time in prayer for those organizations or ministries. Also, take time to talk as a cell to get their real feedback about the activity. A cell needs to do things that the kids in the cell have a heart for.

Although a cell should serve others, don't forget to have time to spend together as a cell. Take time out just to have fun! These times are great for youth to invite their friends to because the setting is relaxed. Youth also need times to wind down and relax. Relationships are the fruit built during fun times as well as serious ones.

"All in all, the most important thing is not to get into a rut with your cell," says Sarah. "I know that is very easy to do, but it is the worst thing that can happen! Keeping youth active and interested are the best ways to do this. Cells are great places for youth to develop good relationships and refuel from rough weeks. Try to have fun with your cell!"

Raising up new leaders

At the end of Julie's senior year of high school, she transferred leadership of the cell to her assistant, Lesley. Lesley had been her assistant for quite some time, helping Julie plan activities, make phone calls, and help in the cell meeting by teaching or leading prayer times.

> "Cells are great places for youth to develop good relationships and refuel from rough weeks," says Sarah.

"Changing leadership could have been a confusing, tumultuous time for the cell, but God's grace was truly with us," says Julie. One of the first things they did was to take the time to communicate about the changes that were going to take place. The leaders heard the kids' concerns and prayed with them so they felt that they were involved in the decision, too. They explained that the cell would change under new leadership but change can be healthy and exciting.

Julie learned that she had to let go of her previous leadership role in the cell. She remained a member of the cell but had to relinquish her role as the "one in charge." Now Julie was the supporter and encourager. By staying in the group, she set the example for the other kids by respecting Lesley and supporting her decisions. "The goal was not to make Lesley a carbon copy of myself," says Julie, "but to encourage her to grow into the leader God had called her to be."

And that's what cell group ministry is about! Cell group ministry works with any age group to grow leaders from the ground up.

A place to fit in

When I was looking for a church, young adult ministry seemed to be missing from many I visited. I found what I was looking for in the cell-based church I now attend. Being part of a young adult cell group really helped me to grow relationships quickly and feel plugged into the church. Now I lead a cell group with my husband.

CHAPTER 14
Post High Ministry:
What About the Xers?

A recent conversation with a group of youth leaders in their twenties was revealing for a youth pastor. He talked with them for hours, as they shared their hopes and frustrations. We believe the essence of what was said is important, so we included it here in this chapter.

This post high age group, (ages 20-35, and dubbed "Baby Busters" or "GenXers" by the media) is looking for their niche. They are the children of the Baby Boomers generation, many growing up as latchkey children while both their boomer parents were working. Out of necessity, they are a self-reliant group, and often feel they don't fit into the existing churches. Although they serve and get involved, they are not really selling out and willing to "put all their eggs in one basket." However, they do want the wisdom and the endorsement of the previous generation for themselves.

They feel that the church has lowered its standards to increase the numbers. They see it as a club, not a community. They want to find the ultimate meaning of life...what God has created them for— what will work for them on a long-term basis. There is something in their hearts that is yet to be birthed: "We don't know what it is, but we do know what it is not!" one Xer told me. Comments like this frustrate and threaten the Baby Boomers who still see themselves as having things basically worked out, thanks to a leftover belief in modernism.

The Boomers expect the Xers to rise up and seize leadership forcefully like they did. The Boomers rose to prominence in society by thrusting themselves violently into the limelight. They were like a newborn baby...born crying and screaming for attention. There were riots, protests and revolution along with psychedelic drugs and rock music.

But the Xers just don't have this in them. They see the mess that has been left behind by the Baby Boomers and are asking, "Isn't there a better way?" They don't see any solutions just around the corner. Business and frenzied activity does not impress them. They want real answers, real families, real communities and real churches that work.

Is this something God has placed in their hearts? We believe it is. The existing church must endorse and support them. If not, the church will lose them, either to mediocrity or to some other thing that will gain their hearts. We must give them the opportunity to create ministry in the church that is uniquely their expression of Christ.

Here, potentially is a great missions and church planting force. They will probably redefine some parameters of leadership and "church" as we know it. But it will be worth the risk required to see this group take up the mantle their generation carries for the kingdom of God.

Church as they "do it" will look different from what we are familiar with, and this is fine. In the future, there probably will be youth/young adult churches that will fill a vacuum created by inflexible current church structures.

Holy tension

One way to get this mobile age group involved is to help them discover in cell groups what they so highly value—intimacy and relationship. Although a post high cell group can offer meaningful and deep relationships, it is always a challenge to keep the aspect of evangelism and outreach within the fabric of the group. It is this tension that keeps the group vibrant and alive. Usually you will find there are a few who are evangelistically gifted. Their ideas and motivation can stir up the group and challenge their inwardness.

A group of young adults will take far less motivation, but far more relationship than a younger group. Many of them, although relatively adult in most aspects of their lives, are new at decision-making and still feel a strong need for godly input from others. Many in this group have already gone through some major life-changing experiences.

Although they may appear "together," some have been hurt in relationships and are still struggling. Bitterness, disappointments and resentments can interrupt relationships they currently have. It can be difficult to break through the shell that they have placed around their hearts. Once the trust and relationship is built with you as a leader, there will be open doors to minister life to those individuals. This first step will help them become more open within the group to talk through issues with others and to minister to each other.

This can be a fast-paced growth period in their lives. Although strong leadership is important, a clear vision is vital. Without those two factors, the group will quickly become so ingrown that it no longer welcomes new people, nor does it allow for much more spiritual growth. The focus can remain on their problems and their relationships with the opposite sex. But with the proper balance, these young people can be great youth cell leaders with much to give.

> Cell groups can help a far away student still feel connected to the church and friends back home.

Maintain contact with college students

Cell groups can play an important part of a far away student still feeling connected to the church and their friends back home. Relationships can be strengthened by treating him as though he was a missionary.

The cell group could help a college cell member(s) move into dorm life. Plan a little party after the meeting. Have everyone bring supplies such as pens, stamps, quarters for laundry, microwave popcorn, etc. You might want to sneak a call in to the student's parents to find out specific needs.

A final exam "goodie box" has always been a hit. Include encouraging notes with the snacks and trinkets that say, "We care!"

Continue to pray for the college students from the cell group. They face many challenges, especially if they are living away from home and Christian friends. Take turns writing letters and sending e-mails.

God bless as you cultivate youth cells!

Whether you have vision for post high, senior high or junior high ages, the values put forth in this book will help you implement effective youth cell ministry. Take time now to pray, and maybe fast, to see how the Lord wants you to begin to apply what you have learned in this book. We will be praying for you as you labor to reach and touch the postmodern generations with the love of God.

APPENDIX
Tools for Your
Youth Cell Groups

Time with God

These steps are intended to help you develop a consistent and effective quiet time. You need to work out the time, place, and way in which you can best develop your relationship with the Lord. Don't feel you have to stick to this pattern completely.

- Use a Bible with good size print in a translation you can easily understand.

- Have a special notebook to keep a record of God's activity in your life and relationships. It is a good tool to help you work through feelings, confront fears, and weigh decisions. Record your prayers and answers.

- Set a specific place. Have an expectancy that God is going to meet with you. Don't rush or hurry.

GUIDELINES

1 **Review what happened yesterday.** Write how you thought it affected your day. Be honest with God and yourself.
- Did you make good decisions or bad decisions?
- Did you use your time wisely or waste it?
- Should you have done anything differently?

2 **Worship** Paraphrase a psalm, write a poem, sing to the Lord either your own song or one that you know. Focus on the things of God that make Him so awesome and worthy of your praise. Be creative.

3 **Confession** If you know of specific sins, ask for giveness for them. Deal with those things before God and experience His forgiveness remembering that you need to turn away from your sin.

4 **Thanksgiving** Express your thanks to the Lord for every thing He has done for you. Thank God for answered prayers and specific blessings. Be motivated to continue worshiping.

5 **Requests** Philippians 4:6. Pray as the Spirit leads.
• The church and church leaders
• People—friends both Christian and non-Christian
• Family and your role within that family
• Personal—Pray about your character, attitudes

6 **Listening to God** Ask these questions and see what the Spirit of God would say:
• What is the next step in my relationship with You?
• What is the next step in the development of my character?
• What is the next step in my family life?
• What is the next step in my ministry? (church, family, friends: we all have a ministry!)

7 **Reading** Come to the Bible reverently, systematically and in-telligently. Don't use your Bible like a promise book. Read up to one chapter, at least until you come across something that sticks out to you. Read it through several times.

8 **Meditating** Ask yourself questions like:
• Is there a promise for me to claim?
• Is there any experience for me to enjoy?
• Is there any sin for me to turn away from?
• Is there a command for me to obey?
• What is God saying to me?
• Is there some new thought about Jesus or His life?
• What is God's message for me today?

9 **Write it down.** Put your thoughts into words. Write down a paragraph about what God has shown you. Pray and adjust your life accordingly.

10 **Share** Tell others in your cell group or even pre-Chris-tians about what you have learned.

11 **Obey!** Put what God shows you into practice. James 1:22. Expect that as you obey, God will reveal more to you!

Sharing Your Testimony

Apostle Paul set an example for us by taking advantage of many opportunities to share his testimony with others. One of these times is recorded in Acts when Paul was speaking to King Agrippa. These verses show a clear pattern to use when we share our own testimonies. Read the whole story in Acts 26:4-23.

1. Before

Again read Acts 26:4-11. Paul's story before meeting Christ

2. Coming to know Christ

Read Acts 26:12-18 Paul's conversion story.

3. What changed

Read Acts 26:19-23. These scriptures talk about how Paul's life changed after his conversion.

How does it work for me?

There are needs in everyone's life, from the history teacher at your school to the guy next door. People need to hear that we have experienced some of the same needs they have. They need to hear how God met those needs in our lives.

You may think your testimony isn't nearly as exciting as Paul's or the next person's. No matter what, your testimony is a powerful way to share truth with others. It's okay to share something simple. You could share some specific problem God helped you overcome.

Take the three steps and tell your experience:

1. Before salvation (what you were like before)
2. Coming to know Christ (how did it happen?)
3. What changed (how was your life different)

P.S. As you share, don't use "religious" terms, such as born again or washed in the blood, etc. Find a way to explain what you want to communicate without speaking "another language."

Evangelism
Approach Questions

Start a spiritual discussion with pre-Christians.

Set #1

1. Have you ever given much thought to the Christian way of life?

2. If someone were to ask you what a real Christian was, what would you say?

3. Have you thought much about your own need of salvation?

4. What do you think a person needs to do to be saved?

5. How do you actually go about receiving eternal life?

6. Can I show you three or four verses from the Bible that show this simply?

Set #2

1. Are you interested in spiritual things?

2. Have you ever considered becoming a real Christian?

3. If someone were to ask you what a real Christian was, what would you tell them?

4. Do you know of any reason why you wouldn't want to invite Jesus into your life right now and become a real Christian?

Set #3

1. Do you feel you know God personally or are you still unsure who God really is?

2. If you died today and stood before God, and the Lord asked you, "Why should I let you into My heaven?" what would you tell Him?

SEX
Ten Reasons to Wait for Marriage
BY LARRY KREIDER

God has an awesome plan for your life! His plans for you are for good, to give you a future and a hope (Jeremiah 29:11). The Lord wants to use you to make a difference in your generation. But the enemy also has a strategy for your life. One of his schemes to destroying God's plan for you is the misuse of sex. Here are ten reasons to wait for marriage.

1 **Because God says so.** Sex is God's idea. Sex is clean and good if we use it according to God's Word, the Bible. Sex was created by God to bring into union a man and woman who have committed their lives together in marriage. You are made of body, soul and spirit. God knows two spirits and souls need to be united through marriage before you can experience the freedom of sex under His plan. What you do with your body touches your spirit. Sex is not just a physical thing. It is a blending of two entire personalities—body, soul and spirit. God calls sexual relationships outside of marriage sin, and tells us that those living in immorality will not inherit the kingdom of God. (I Cor. 6:9-11) God hates sin because it destroys someone He loves, YOU!

2 **To protect you from memories of past relationships.** Another way to say it: to protect you from the "ghosts of relationships past." Those involved in any type of sexual activity before marriage usually have to deal with flashbacks and hurts from past relationships when they get married. The enemy uses these flashbacks to place extra stress and strain on a marriage relationship. We need to renew our minds by the Word of God in order to be set free (Romans 12:1-2).

3 **It protects us from distrust and suspicion** Many married couples struggle in their marriage because they were involved in some type of immoral behavior before they were married. Distrust and suspicion wipe out the basis for intimacy in marriage.

4 **To build a foundation of trust in a relationship.** Good marriages are built on trust, not sex. One of the lies from hell is that you need to have sexual experience before you are married. Sex before marriage destroys the trust that a good sexual relationship is built on. You have your entire life to practice and grow sexually with your marriage partner.

5 **Because purity takes away all fear of disease.** "Two decades after the appearance of HIV, an estimated 30 million people have contracted the virus, and 6 million have died of AIDS. About 90 percent of infections occur in developing countries, where the disease has already reduced life expectancy, in some cases by more than a decade."[1] Anyone involved sexually with someone other than their spouse is having, in reality, sexual relations with each of that person's previous sexual partners.

[1] "Confronting Aids: Public Priorities in a Global Epidemic," <www:worldbank.org/aids-econ/confront/confrontfull/> June 2000.

6 Sexual impurity makes it hard to obey God and hard to break up a relationship. Sex ruins a good relationship or it sustains a bad one. It creates an emotional bond and causes a person to think the relationship is deeper than it really is.

7 Sexual impurity causes the couple's communication and whole relationship to deteriorate. Every good marriage is based on communication. Premarital sex distorts and lessens that communication. By keeping a relationship focused on emotional, intellectual and spiritual levels, good communication has a greater chance of happening. Hollywood tries to make us believe that sex before marriage is normal and healthy. Remember, the actors get paid to do what they do, and in real life, the majority of their marriages end in shambles.

8 God wants to protect you from losing your virginity. One young girl told her peers who were teasing her about being a virgin, "Any day I can become like you. But you can never become like me."

9 To protect your testimony and avoid guilt and condemnation. In II Samuel 12:14, Nathan said to David, "By this deed you have given occasion to the enemies of the Lord to blaspheme me." Nathan told him this after David had committed sexual sin with Bathsheba.

A woman wrote a letter to a past boyfriend asking for forgiveness for sexual promiscuity years before. The Lord set her conscience free through this act of obedience.

10 The seed of sexual activity before marriage will produce a crop of immorality and confusion after marriage (unless you truly repent and the curse is broken in Jesus' name). God's plan is for the sexual act to unite two people who are committed in a marriage relationship. The devil's tactic is to use sex to divide couples before they are married, through immorality, which will produce a lack of trust.

Even after people are married, the enemy often tries to tempt them to become attracted to someone other than their husband or wife. The devil's strategy is always to divide and to destroy. The same disciplines and grace needed before marriage are also needed afterward.

If you have messed up...

If you have committed sexual sin in the past, realize your sin has grieved a Holy God. Confess your sin and receive His cleansing today (I John 1:9).

God's incredible plan for you...

Purpose in your heart that you will maintain a high standard of purity in your life from this day on, saving your sexuality for your husband or wife. The Bible tells us to flee sexual immorality (I Cor. 6:18). In other words, run from it! Find someone who you can be accountable to as you live out your life of purity. Submit yourself to God, resist the devil in Jesus' name, and expect God to use you to change your generation!

Sex and You

Age_____   Male ❑ Female ❑

1. How long have you been a Christian?

2. How much do you know about sex? (A lot, a little, some?)

3. Where did you learn what you know about sex? (school, Mom, Dad, friends, TV and movies, magazines, books)

4. Personally, what standards do you go by while dating?

5. My definition of fornication...

6. Do you think you've ever gone too far?

7. What makes you think you did?

8. Do you feel free and forgiven?

9. What confuses or concerns you about sex and dating?

10. Specifically list steps you can take to prevent sexual impurity while dating.

11. Do you struggle with lust and impure thoughts?

Could This Be the One?

1. Does he/she have a serious commitment to the Lord? Is his/her time with God a high priority? Is your relationship drawing you both closer to the Lord?

2. Is he/she thankful for the way God's made him/her? (Self-acceptance is very important. A poor self-image will result in a dependence on the spouse to continually lift them up).

3. Does he/she have a clean conscience? Has he/she asked forgiveness and made restitution? Is he/she open about the past?

4. How does he/she speak about parents and other authority figures?

5. Is he/she quick to say "I'm sorry"? What is his/her reaction when someone wrongs him/her? How does he/she handle the little problems?

6. Does he/she have clear goals? Do you have similar goals and lifestyles?

7. Has he/she committed his/her finances and earning power to the Lord? Is he/she generous and responsible with money and things ?

8. Is he/she capable of being a good friend—your best friend?

9. Is he/she capable of having lots of fun and being joyful?

10. Can you trust his/her judgment and decision-making?

11. How do you feel about having him/her parent your children?

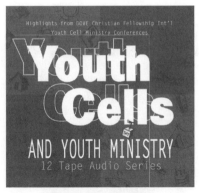

Highlights from DOVE Christian Fellowship Int'l
Youth Cell Ministry Conferences

Youth Cells
AND YOUTH MINISTRY
12 Tape Audio Series

Youth Cells Audio Set

Fresh insights for those just getting started with home cell groups as well as for those who are veterans. These audio tapes are taught by experienced cell leaders and pastors from the DCFI family of churches including Larry and LaVerne Kreider.

Topics
- *Youth Revival*
- *Intimacy with God*
- *Vision*
- *History and Cell Basics*
- *Cell Group Practicals*
- *Traditional Youth Pastor vs. Relational Youth Leader*
- *Motivating Youth to Pray*
- *Motivating Youth to Worship*
- *Father's Heart*
- *Creative Models*
- *Tips for Teen Cell Leaders*
- *Reaching Prophetic Personality Youth*

Youth Cell Group Set: **$45.00**

Youth Cell Ministry Conferences

Today's youth culture values honesty, relationship and community—they are ripe for a youth cell movement. Learn what it takes to train young people in ministry so they can play an active and vital part in the body of Christ.
Designed for those considering youth cells or those looking for new ideas, including teen leaders.

House To House

How a cell group became an international family of cell-based churches. Larry Kreider, draws from two decades worth of victories and defeats to communicate lessons of operating in a new church paradigm. Use as a handbook for cell group dynamics.
By Larry Kreider, 206 pages **$8.95**